A Guide to International Law Careers

Anneke Smit and Christopher Waters

British Institute of
**International and
Comparative Law**

Published and Distributed by
The British Institute of International and Comparative Law
Charles Clore House, 17 Russell Square, London WC1B 5JP

© BIICL 2015

2nd edition

British Library Cataloguing in Publication Data
A Catalogue record of this book is available from the British Library

ISBN 978-1-905221-55-4
e-ISBN 978-1-905221-58-5

Typeset by Cambrian Typesetters
Camberley, Surrey
Printed in Great Britain by
Polestar Wheatons Ltd

For Alies

Table of Contents

Acknowledgements

The authors thank Inesa Buchyn for her research assistance in preparing the second edition of this Guide as well as the numerous students at the Faculty of Law, University of Windsor who provided useful research and comments on the first edition of this Guide. At the British Institute of International and Comparative Law we would like to thank the Director, Robert McCorquodale for his support of this project and for writing the Foreword, and Anna Riddell for her interest in publishing this Guide. Finally, we are grateful to our international law panel members who have provided practitioners' perspectives to this Guide. The authors would be pleased to receive feedback on the Guide; they may be reached at asmit@uwindsor.ca or cwaters@uwindsor.ca.

Foreword

> Without international lawyers, there would have been no international law. From Hugo Grotius to the International Criminal Court, international law has been a *project* carried out by international lawyers. It has been sometimes a religious, sometimes a secular humanitarian project, a project for order, civilization, peace, security, development, rule of law and so on.
>
> Martti Koskenniemi (2007)[1]

International law is one of the great projects (to use Martti Koskenniemi's words above) of the past century. In the course of that time it has moved from containing occasional treaties between absolute sovereigns to having a vast array of international documents, organizations and institutions, and judicial and other dispute settlement bodies, and applying to a range of participants. It is now a legal system with considerable international and national implications.

This dynamic development of international law has required more international lawyers. No longer are international lawyers just a few legal courtiers to the sovereign or an occasional theological scholar with a legal interest. Now international lawyers are found in many corporations, working in refugee camps, managing international financial organizations, on a government trade mission, in transactional and litigation areas of law firms, deciding human rights cases, drafting tax legislation, advising environmental non-governmental organizations, enthusing students at universities, and doing a wide variety of other legal and non-legal jobs. There is a need for international lawyers across the world.

Despite this, there are still uncertainties about what is an international lawyer and what type of career there can be in international law. That is why this book is so essential. The authors, from their own experiences, recognise that there are different careers possible for those who are interested in international law. This book sets out, in a very accessible way, the various careers that are available and deals with the many questions that are asked about a career as an international lawyer. The use of quotes from those practising in the area and direction to places where further information can be obtained is also invaluable.

---

[1] Martti Koskenniemi, 'International Lawyers', talk for the Erik Castrén Institute of International Law and Human Rights, University of Helsinki (2007) [his emphasis]: http://www.helsinki.fi/eci/Publications/MKINTERNATIONAL%20LAWYERS-07b.pdf.

It is most appropriate that this book is published by the British Institute of International and Comparative Law. The Institute is one of the leading independent research centres for international and comparative law in the world. Its membership includes the whole range of international lawyers in the United Kingdom and around the world, from judges of the International Court of Justice to lawyers in non-governmental organizations, from international legal scholars to general counsel of corporations, from government legal advisors to United Nations officials, from legal practitioners to students. All of these people at some time thought about a career in international law.

I commend this book as a wonderful resource for all those who are thinking about a career (or a career change) in international law, for those who are passionate about international law and for those who want to change the world:

The actual is the possible. The function of the new international lawyer is to change the course of human history.

Philip Allott (2005)[2]

Professor Robert McCorquodale
Director
British Institute of International and Comparative Law

---

[2] Philip Allott, *Towards the International Rule of Law* (London: Cameron May, 2005), 463.

Preface

The experience of many students studying public international law at university is, 'This is fascinating, but what can I do with it?' While this Guide in no way detracts from the more intangible reasons to study international law – from being a better-informed global citizen to relieving the parochialism and insularity of the traditional, domestic-focused law curriculum – it is practically focused. The essential message is that international law jobs are out there and attainable if approached strategically and with perseverance. The Guide was written partly out of the authors' frustration that so much of the career material disseminated by law school careers advisors, or in mainstream legal publications targeted at students, pushes one career stream: becoming a barrister or solicitor and practicing domestic law (though even here, as we will highlight, there is large scope for using international law). Our hope is that this short reference book will prompt serious – because pursuing a job in this area is not for the faint-hearted – students to consider a career in the area of international law. If you are one of these students, we also hope that it will give you some tools for carving out a career path. As a preliminary point, we should note that the Guide focuses primarily on careers with a significant public international law component as opposed to careers centred on international business transactions or private international law. We hasten to add though that the boundaries between these areas have eroded in recent years.

A note on the format is also in order. The Guide is written as a dialogue between aspiring international lawyers and the authors. Rather than a product of pure invention however, these dialogues replicate the dialogues international law teachers will have had with their students countless times. The dialogue is supplemented in two ways. First, we have assembled a panel of international lawyers practicing in a variety of areas of international law to provide commentary and reflect on personal experiences with the various topics addressed in the Guide. These 'practitioners' voices' are interspersed throughout the text. We hope these will give you a direct sense of the diversity of jobs international lawyers do and what the lawyers' career paths have looked like. The approaches and advice offered by practitioners are not always consistent with one another – or indeed with our views – but we consider this diversity of views to be one of the Guide's strengths, since there is no 'one size fits all' approach. Second, appendices are included which provide you with hard, factual information on the courses and internships which are the stepping stones to international law jobs, as well as web links to allow you to access the most up-to-date information. The information supplied in these appendices is indicative of what is available rather than being comprehensive and does not do away with the need to 'dig' to find the course, internship or position which is right for you. The Guide and the appendices are broadly aimed at British and Commonwealth students but we trust that students from other jurisdictions will also find them useful given the dearth of similar resources.

There is a wide variety of potential jobs in international law, or with international law as a significant component. Among the employers of international law specialists are international organizations, regional organizations, non-governmental organizations, government departments, law firms and universities. The jobs that are out there can take countless forms, from something resembling traditional legal practice (courtroom advocacy and drafting) to monitoring human rights in the field (literally at times). As the ambit of international law increases (or as some writers have suggested, world politics become 'legalised') so too the number of jobs grows. This Guide is intended to help you consider whether such a career is right for you and how you can develop an international law practice should the answer to that question be 'yes'.

1

The Employers

What employers should I be looking at?

The range of potential employers in international law is vast. This chapter breaks it down employer by employer, to help you get a sense of where your skills, interests and personality might be best placed.

Basic subcategories of employers are: international organizations (organizations formed primarily by states), international courts and tribunals, non-governmental organizations (NGOs), government departments, law firms and universities. The numbers of these employers are not insignificant. It is estimated that there are over 450 international organizations, and there is a growing number of international courts and tribunals established under the aegis of international organizations or by separate treaty. There are literally thousands of NGOs with an international law dimension to their work. Every central government hires international lawyers. While there are few law firms which do public international law exclusively, increasing numbers of law firms have significant public international law dimensions to their practices. Finally, while this may not always have been the case, it is now inconceivable to have a credible law programme at a university without offering public international law as a course option. Increasing numbers of law schools are even making public international law a mandatory course, meaning academia is likely a growth area for international lawyers.

Which international organizations should I consider?

When people think about practising law with an international organization, they immediately tend to think of the United Nations (UN). This makes sense. The UN proper employs hundreds of international lawyers. The various branches of the UN 'family', often ignored by inexperienced job seekers, hire hundreds more. So, for example, while some people will be employed directly by an organ of the UN – say working for the Department of Peacekeeping Operations or the Office of Legal Affairs in the UN Secretariat – others will be employed by specialised programmes and agencies such as the UN Environment Programme (UNEP) or the UN High Commissioner for Refugees (UNHCR).

1

I would encourage all students to consider working for the UN even if for a short time.

Working for the UN has allowed me to contribute to its key mandate of service to humanity, in an environment of respect for diversity, as well as personal and professional integrity. Those who find these values important will also find working for the UN very fulfilling. In addition, the UN provides an unrivalled opportunity for young lawyers to interact with colleagues from a broad range of cultural, linguistic and social backgrounds and to learn from these experiences. It is therefore a good place for young lawyers to grow both professionally and personally.

However there are also shortcomings. Except for New York, Geneva, or Vienna, most offices and activities are located in developing and transition economies. Working for the UN may therefore require relocation to distant, often remote, corners of the world with few or no modern facilities, and fairly spartan living conditions. In addition, some of the duty stations are in conflict or post-conflict zones, raising security concerns. For example, my work for the UN over the past ten years has taken me to Rwanda, Tanzania, Sierra Leone, Afghanistan, and now South Sudan!

Another thing worth mentioning is the somewhat bureaucratic nature of the organization. Almost everything that needs to be done is usually subject to several layers of administrative approval.

> *Alhagi Marong*, Legal Affairs Officer, United Nations
> Mission in South Sudan (UNMISS), Juba, South Sudan

I worked as an intern at UN headquarters doing research on Security Council decisions and then several years later at UNESCO on political affairs. The advantages for someone interested in international law were exposure to decision-making processes within the UN system and first-hand experience with understanding conflicting priorities and concerns of delegates from different member states. One disadvantage of working within large organisations was the lengthiness of processes even in getting day-to-day work signed off.

> *Xiao Hui Eng*, Research Fellow in Citizenship Education
> and the Rule of Law, Bingham Centre for the Rule of Law,
> BIICL, London

We'll come back to what kinds of jobs you can get within the UN, but for now let's go on to regional organizations.

In Europe there are several regional organizations. The European Union (EU) is the most prominent of these. As every British law student can tell you, the EU is not a purely international organization. It is supranational and, to use a favourite phrase of international lawyers, *sui generis*. Nonetheless, the treaties which form the EU are international treaties, and international law principles continue to govern relations between the EU and its member states and between member states. Furthermore, the EU is an international actor, in terms of trade and also, increasingly, in areas such as international peace and security and development. Like the UN, there are numerous different branches and sectors of law within which one can work in the EU. Careers advisors in the UK typically have more information on careers in the EU than on any other sort of international law career. Also, career paths in the EU are more defined and information is readily obtainable from the web and other sources. If you are a law student elsewhere in the Commonwealth, the EU will likely be less relevant to you as an employer (although see our note on citizenship below).

The other major European organization which employs lawyers is the Council of Europe, headquartered in Strasbourg, France. Given the Council of Europe's emphasis on human rights and democratization, lawyers are key to many of its operations and not only in the context of the Council's judicial branch (namely, the European Court of Human Rights, which will be familiar to law students). With a broad definition of Europe, including Turkey, there are now 47 states in the Council of Europe.

A third 'European' organization to mention is the Organization for Security for Cooperation in Europe (OSCE). The OSCE's mandate includes a range of security-related concerns, including confidence-building measures, human rights, minorities, democratization and policing. Despite its name, the organization's 57 member states include Canada and the US as well as all the former Soviet States, due to its origins as a Cold War forum for dialogue. The OSCE does hire some people directly, both at its headquarters in Vienna and at the Office of Democratic Institutions and Human Rights (ODIHR – pronounced 'oh dear') in Warsaw. ODIHR hires legal advisers to work on its many election monitoring missions in the field as well. However, most people working for the OSCE are actually 'seconded', which means that they are formally loaned to the organization for a specific mission by the government of a member state. Some countries, including Canada and Britain, have provided particularly large contingents of secondees to the OSCE, including to the Ukraine electoral missions in 2014.

Outside of Europe, major regional organizations include the Organization of American States (OAS) and the African Union (AU). These organizations hire lawyers for work in their secretariats, as well as for thematically focused organs or programmes. For example, the Inter-American Commission on Human Rights and the African Commission on Human and People's Rights offer opportunities to work in human rights. There is no comprehensive pan-Asian organization but there are several sector-specific or sub-regional organizations and institutions, such as the Asian Development Bank (which hires both 'in house' lawyers and consultants for delivery of the Bank's technical assistance programmes) and the Association of Southeast Asian Nations

(ASEAN). The Commonwealth, which is sometimes also placed in the category of 'regional organizations', is a source of potential employment for Commonwealth citizens, in particular through the Rule of Law Division of the Commonwealth Secretariat.

Usually regional organizations hire only nationals of member states, at least as full-time staff (internships and consulting positions are more open), but if you do some family tree research you may find a way to qualify for citizenship of an organization's member state and therefore access these jobs. The same goes for certain UN jobs, for which there is a quota system to ensure equitable geographic selection of staff.

Some international organizations, rather than having a comprehensive mandate, focus on a specific theme or purpose. These range from relatively unknown organizations, like the International Copper Study Group or the International Pacific Halibut Commission, to 'household name' international organizations such as the World Health Organization (WHO) or the World Food Programme (WFP) which has been particularly active recently in places such as Syria and South Sudan. Another well-known organization is the International Committee of the Red Cross (ICRC), with its mandate as the guardian of international humanitarian law (IHL or the law of armed conflict as it is sometimes called). The ICRC is actually a tricky one to classify, since it has components of both an international organization and an NGO. This so-called 'hybrid' institution, while given a mandate by international treaties, is run by a board of private citizens. The ICRC hires people directly from around the world, sometimes with the assistance of national Red Cross and Red Crescent Societies.

> The advantages of working with the ICRC include a relatively steady job and the possibility of interesting legal work in various parts of the world. The organization is well-run and stable. There is a good working atmosphere in most of the delegations, while the type of work is varied and touches on some of the 'big issues' of the day, including International Humanitarian Law (IHL or the law of armed conflict) and its relationship to human rights law, and the regulation of the responses to terrorist acts.
>
> The disadvantage (if it can be seen as such) is that the work concentrates on IHL, which has two limitations. First, many of the problems of the people and countries covered cannot be solved directly by IHL. Second, IHL applies only in times of armed conflict, which limits work in areas which could use much help but are not in a situation of armed conflict. However, the ICRC also works (with state consent) in some parts of the world which may be called "other situations of violence" if the test for armed conflict is not met.
>
> The ICRC's efforts as a whole include areas as varied as providing clean water solutions, family reunification, detention visits, and work with

national Red Cross and Red Crescent societies, in addition to legal work relating to the 1949 Geneva Conventions and their Additional Protocols. Legal work in the field often involves not only IHL-related work, but also varied requests from the delegations.

Christopher Harland, Legal Adviser, Regional Delegation for the United States and Canada, ICRC, Washington, DC

Is court work at the international level an achievable goal?

Yes. International adjudication generally is an expanding area. Some fields, in particular international criminal justice, have seen explosive growth. Starting in 1993 with the establishment of the International Criminal Tribunal for the former Yugoslavia (ICTY) there has been a massive increase in the number of lawyers employed in international criminal law. The ICTY has been joined by the International Criminal Tribunal for Rwanda (ICTR) and several so-called hybrid tribunals (mixing international and domestic judges) in places including Kosovo, Sierra Leone, Cambodia and Lebanon. The International Criminal Court (ICC) came into existence in 2002 and has already handed down some preliminary decisions. The ICC alone has three principal organs – Chambers, Office of the Prosecutor and the Registry – which are all potential sources of employment. Aside from international criminal law, there are many other courts and tribunals adjudicating on matters such as trade, intellectual property and the law of the sea, which offer employment to lawyers.

One of the primary advantages of working for an international tribunal such as the Special Tribunal for Lebanon or the ICTY is gaining valuable experience in the field of international criminal law. There are fascinating, novel legal issues to be addressed. The work is conducted in an international legal environment which combines concepts from different legal systems such as the common law and civil law. There is the opportunity to work with and learn from lawyers, analysts and investigators from around the world. There is also the possibility of doing field work, primarily related to investigations.

Many of the international tribunals are not permanent. For example, the ICTY is an ad hoc institution, created by a Security Council Resolution under Chapter VII of the UN Charter. As an ad hoc institution, the staff employees are not long term staff of the UN but are on short term UN contracts that can be renewed on a yearly basis. Because of this, employment at the ICTY does not result in a contract with the United Nations Secretariat, but with the ICTY only. As such, persons who wish to work for the ICTY need to be aware that it is limited in its time frame. It is also in a downsizing phase, completing its final trials and appeals. Eventually staff will need to find other jobs when the Tribunal and its residual office close its doors. The International Criminal Court, being a more long term institution, may give longer term contracts and is expected to continue after the ad hoc tribunals or short term international or hybrid criminal courts finish their mandates. Persons who are interested in a career in international criminal law need to keep this in mind.

Norman Farrell, Prosecutor,
Special Tribunal for Lebanon, The Hague

Less obvious to job seekers, perhaps, are non-criminal ad hoc tribunals, such as the Kosovo Property Agency (adjudicating housing and property claims) or international commissions of inquiry. While many employees, including legal staff, are locally trained and qualified, these tribunals also employ international lawyers and adjudicators. International lawyers who have significant domestic legal experience in the subject matter of a tribunal will be particularly attractive candidates, as will be touched upon in Chapter 3.

I've always thought of myself as an 'NGO type'. But can you actually get a paying job with these not-for-profit organizations?

NGOs range from small organizations, operating at a purely local level, to large transnational organizations such as Amnesty International or Friends of the Earth. NGOs form the core of what is known as 'civil society' and are crucial elements of a healthy and rule of law-oriented society. Of course not all NGOs are involved with international law, but those that are have been increasingly active in recent years in monitoring state compliance with international law, and indeed seeking to change the law itself, through activism and lobbying. Volunteers are often at the heart of an NGO's activities, but most also rely on paid employees including staff lawyers. So yes, the NGO sector is definitely a place to look for work in international law.

There are many advantages of working for an NGO like Human Rights Watch. Being based in New York in a well-known organization affords access to high-level officials – including diplomats and senior UN officials – that I never had while I worked for the United Nations, for example. As a result, we are able to put forward our human rights concerns (gathered through our own research and in conjunction with our local NGO partners on the ground) much more efficiently and effectively. We also work closely with journalists and media outlets around the world to present our targeted recommendations to a broader audience so as to influence public opinion, including policy makers. This is one of the ways Human Rights Watch – through its staff – is able to move policy debates around key human rights issues towards human rights goals, and therefore affect change.

Being part of such a dynamic process is something I had not previously experienced working for the government or the United Nations. I have definitely developed skills that I never would have used in my previous jobs and which are not necessarily typical for more mainstream jobs in law, such as how to handle tough meetings with diplomats, the best way to make advocacy points during radio and television interviews, and how to create a strategy to create pressure on policy makers in order realize a particular outcome.

Param-Preet Singh, Senior Counsel, International Justice Program, Human Rights Watch, New York

I have worked in domestic and international NGOs doing research on both international law-related issues and on some aspects of domestic human rights law. I found that an advantage of working in smaller NGOs was the chance to make significant contributions. There is always more work to do than there is staff to do it, so I was given the opportunity to manage whole portfolios and to work quite independently. I would say that a disadvantage of working for some of the smaller NGOs is the need for constant pursuit of funding which means that work and contracts may be dependent on success with obtaining funding.

Xiao Hui Eng, Research Fellow in Citizenship Education and the Rule of Law, Bingham Centre for the Rule of Law, BIICL, London

We are an international NGO working in the area of human rights and governance. We research and advocate for systemic change/improvement/reform in the areas of access to justice and access to information. If I were a newbie I'd say the disadvantage of working with us is the wage. It is low for a law grad, especially one who has to pay off loans. There is also the huge question of ego. People feel – and often can't get over – the societal pressure of their peers earning more. They vacillate between their so called 'commitment' and the desire (rather than the need) to earn well. I wanted to mention this because it has come up so often in interviews. I see the struggle and have to refrain from saying that if there is genuine commitment and passion one tempers one's ego and financial expectations so that you can be devoted to your work. But that is an aside. The advantages of being in an organisation like ours are boundless for the newcomer. Newcomers are given research and advocacy tasks, deliberate mentoring, helped with writing, and encouraged to take over other people's foundational work and take it forward. For the curious and the self-starter there is everything to gain in terms of book learning, real life experience of policy making at the highest levels and network and contacts. Demonstrably, the clever and the ambitious have used our space to improve their prospects while learning skills and meeting folks and there is a free hand given to do this within the parameters of one's duties. I also feel that there is a certain level of professional behaviour and ethics learned here that stands our staff in good stead.

Maja Daruwala, Director,
Commonwealth Human Rights Initiative, New Delhi

Sometimes NGOs will gather together in networks, pooling resources and adopting common positions. These networks themselves also provide opportunities for employment. An example of this is the Coalition for the International Criminal Court (CICC), an umbrella organization of more than 2500 NGOs. Some countries, notably Nordic and Western European countries including Germany and the Netherlands, also host NGOs with ties to the state. Although given a good deal of operational independence, their funding and mandate may be state-driven. These are sometimes known as Quasi-NGOs, or QANGOs (pronounced 'kwangos'). Germany's Friedrich Ebert Stiftung is one example.

What about jobs in the domestic civil service?

Every country has a foreign ministry which hires lawyers, usually from among its own citizens. These may be legal advisers whose sole task is to provide international law advice to the government. In the UK the Foreign and Commonwealth Office employs about 50 Legal Advisers in London, with a handful of Legal Advisers posted overseas in places such as New York, Geneva and Brussels. Lawyers may also work as diplomats who bring with them their legal training and skills. In both cases selection and training tend to be rigorous and the competition for these posts is high.

A foreign service legal career offers a unique opportunity to practice in a wide range of areas of international law. In a typical career, you will rotate areas of specialization each few years and you will have the opportunity to practice overseas on postings. I advised on issues from immunities and recognition of states to use of force and compliance with the laws of armed conflict. As your advice feeds into policy making and practice, you are also well placed to influence the implementation and development of international law.

Gavin Hood, Former Legal Adviser,
UK Foreign and Commonwealth Office, Washington

Working for a government ministry such as Canada's Department of Foreign Affairs, Trade and Development offers a number of advantages. First, the opportunities to work on public international law issues are unparalleled. While private sector lawyers can find niche international law practices, the breadth of opportunity to negotiate and draft treaties and work on international trade and dispute resolution, human rights, law of armed force, international environmental law, just to name a few areas of practice, is highest in government. Second, government lawyers usually have the opportunity to move through different branches of law and/or, depending on one's career track, to move to embassies in different countries. Third, while salaries are lower than in the private sector, there is usually greater stability of employment and a better work-life balance. Finally, the opportunity to represent one's country cannot be underestimated – public service is an honourable calling and there is an intangible but deep satisfaction derived from being a government lawyer.

Mark Luz, Counsel and Acting Deputy Director,
Trade Law Bureau, Canadian Department of Foreign Affairs,
Trade and Development, Ottawa

In my role as a Government legal adviser, speaking in general terms the kinds of international law issues I encountered routinely included issues relating to the interpretation, application and analysis of international human rights law, international humanitarian law, the law on the use of force, international refugee law and diverse areas of international security law. My work commonly involved issues relating to the law of treaties, jurisdiction and state responsibility. My work would also often involve issues relating to the development of new international law, and the application of existing international law to novel situations. It would also encompass the management of projects relating to the Government's domestic implementation of its international law obligations (such as the development of legislation), and work related to the Government's obligations to report to international bodies, or to participate in multilateral or bilateral meetings.

I loved the range of interesting international law work involved, and the opportunities provided to move between different roles and to diversify my knowledge. I enjoyed the combination of deep, analytical legal work, practical problem-solving and engagement with a diverse range of stakeholders. I liked the fast-paced work environment, but also the opportunities to work on longer-term legal projects. I appreciated the opportunity to work with and learn from very senior, more experienced international lawyers in Government and valued working in the public service – feeling that my work would ultimately have some form of real-world impact. I also really valued other aspects of working in the public service, such as the strong public service ethics; the good working conditions, and the many opportunities provided to develop one's broader skills, for example in leadership, people management, project management, communication, negotiation and strategic thinking.

Sarah McCosker, Legal Adviser, International Committee of
the Red Cross, Geneva (Formerly Principal Legal Officer,
Office of International Law, Attorney-General's Department,
Australian Government, Canberra)

There are also many jobs in international law with government outside of foreign offices. For example, the UK's Department for International Development (DFID) is involved in a number of rule of law development projects around the world, many of which are implemented through its dozens of overseas offices. Similarly, lawyers in the UK's Home Office, when dealing with asylum matters, may be required to have a strong familiarity with international refugee law. A Canadian example is the federal government's Department of Justice War Crimes Unit, which prosecutes international crimes such as genocide. Ministries of trade will also hire legal advisors to deal with matters that may arise under international trade law – such as resolving disputes in the context of the World Trade Organization (WTO) or negotiating a bilateral free trade agreement – or engaging in arbitration under investment treaties.

I have worked for government, the ICRC and NGOs. An advantage of working on international law in a governmental environment is that you are at the heart of international law issues. International law primarily concerns States; and it is States that regulate and develop international law, so working for government you are at the forefront of international law implementation and development. Also, policy experience in international law is invaluable if applying for a UN or other international organisation job eventually. One disadvantage, however, is that you will always be applying and working along the lines of the policy objectives determined by the government of the day – you will have little opportunity in your first years at least, to influence policy or be at all activist.

Working for an NGO, on the other hand, you can be an activist – you can promote your own values and views (as long as you choose an NGO that accords with your personal views). A disadvantage of the NGO activist world, however, is that sometimes the people within the organizations become so attached to their particular slant on an international law perspective that they are unwilling to accept new interpretations from newcomers. This can end up placing you in the same situation as the government job, where you have to toe the NGO's policy line. Without these restrictions, however, in an NGO world, you can often be more creative and flexible with interpretations of international law than you could ever be in government – and you might get to see the practical results of your work helping people.

Kelisiana Thynne, Research Manager, Australian Civil-Military Centre, Queanbeyan, New South Wales

Often overlooked but growing in importance are legal advisers to the military. These may be civilian legal advisers working for ministries of defence, or uniformed lawyers – in some Commonwealth countries called Judge Advocate General (JAG) Officers – who provide direct operational advice to commanders on international law matters. Legal advisers are increasingly being deployed in the field.

Is all international employment in the public sector?

While we know of only two law firms or chambers of any size doing solely public international law (Volterra Fietta and Three Crowns in London), there are several whose practices have strong international law components, and this list is growing. Lawyers in these practices may act on behalf of private clients seeking redress against governments for acts such as torture. Not infrequently this type of human rights work on behalf of individuals will be on a reduced fee, *pro bono* or legal aid basis. More lucratively, lawyers also represent states before international tribunals. Then there are the corporate-commercial firms with a prominent international trade law practice (litigating rights and responsibilities under international trading regimes such as the World Trade Organization or the North American Free Trade Agreement) and there are numerous public international law issues which arise in a globalised business and investment oriented practice (such as litigating cases under Bilateral Investment Treaties). Questions of immunities may arise in state-investor disputes for example, and issues concerning labour or environmental standards may arise in transnational manufacturing contracts. Some of these matters are handled by in-house counsel of transnational corporations, another source of potential employment. Finally it should be noted that as international law arguments are increasingly being raised before domestic courts on matters ranging from international adoption to human rights, so there are very few areas of domestic legal practice where international law issues will never arise (although many poorly trained lawyers still fail to spot these issues).

Cases arise at the Bar in a number of different fields. Many come up in the public law area – extradition, asylum, and human rights all yield many points of international law. So, too, do commercial cases. WTO issues, investment protection and economic sanctions all appear before domestic courts and are part of the bread-and-butter of international lawyers at the Bar. Then there is the category of 'pure' international law issues: land and maritime boundary disputes, treaty questions, issues of statehood and all of the other subjects that arise in the International Court of Justice and other international tribunals.

The first two of those categories – public law and commercial law cases with an international element – tend to point lawyers to one or other of the few sets of chambers with a serious specialization in international law. Work in the third, 'pure international law', category generally seeks out a suitable international lawyer wherever he or she may be.

Vaughan Lowe QC, Barrister, Essex Court Chambers;
Emeritus Professor of Public International Law,
Emeritus Fellow of All Souls College, Oxford University

I enjoy being at the heart of international law and its development. I work on cases which are not only intellectually interesting and challenging, but also have the potential to make a very real difference to the lives of my clients and those of their families. One of our cases also led to institutional changes at the UN level; the UN Ombudsperson procedure was introduced by the UN Security Council after the ECJ annulled sanctions imposed in the EU to implement UN sanctions.

Miranda Rushton, Senior Associate, Carter-Ruck Solicitors, London

Look for companies that have demonstrated a meaningful commitment to human rights, including through a human rights policy. If you're going to succeed in a role that concentrates on helping the company to implement international human rights standards you will need to look for an employer that is truly going to support this work. Think about the human rights issues in which you have the greatest interest and look for industries that may deal with those issues – for instance, if you're interested in the right to privacy and freedom of expression you might look for an internet or telecommunications company, or if you're interested in the rights of indigenous peoples you might look at working for an extractives company.

Vanessa Zimmerman, Human Rights and Business
Specialist in the Resource Sector

What about jobs in academia?

International law is taking an ever more prominent place in the law school curriculum across the Commonwealth and indeed around the world. This is true at both the undergraduate and post-graduate levels. Law schools are increasingly bringing a transnational orientation to their offerings and most will have at least a few international legal academics on staff. International legal academics also engage in consulting for governments, international organizations, and NGOs, and some senior international law academics are much sought after as advocates before international courts. Indeed the current and previous British judges on the ICJ were both academic-practitioners prior to their appointment to the bench. Some strong international law clinics at universities are also emerging – particularly in the United States – though the UK is somewhat behind in this trend.

Among the advantages of doing international law from the academy, and there are several including relative flexibility over time, is the ability to champion unpopular views. Unlike lawyers working for other public sector employers, academics do not have to have their writing vetted by their superiors. Academic freedom also includes the freedom to tackle 'big issues' and challenge the activities of powerful actors. For a good sense of the evolving job market for legal scholars and teachers in the UK, regularly follow the postings at http://www.jobs.ac.uk.

Some of the advantages of the academic career path include being able to work relatively independently in terms of planning your teaching and research, to express critical views and to train the next generation of international lawyers, some of whom may follow in your footsteps, or even better you in their professional achievements! Some of the disadvantages may include the development of an overwhelming dependency on the academy for many of your views – sometimes to the detriment of knowing how international law is actually applied in practice. Occasionally, there may be difficulty in networking effectively within a broader cross-section of international lawyers drawn from areas other than academia such as government and private practice.

Mary Footer, Professor of International Economic Law,
University of Nottingham

The academic life has huge benefits. Probably the most obvious of these is flexibility of time. It can be a high pressure job that can involve long hours, but – aside from making your classes and certain administrative meetings – how you organise your time is largely up to you. The role is a 'task-based' one; so you 'need to do what you need to do' in terms of balancing your research, your teaching and your administrative responsibilities in your law school. This can mean it is hard to switch off, because you don't necessarily 'punch out' at the end of the day as with many jobs (sometimes you simply *can't* because of a class the next day you've not had time to prepare for or an imminent publication deadline, or whatever it may be). However, it is often possible within the working week to make time for other things – whether it's going to the bank, spending time with the kids or just taking a break – so long as you get everything done at other times. That is such a luxury. The flipside of this, of course, is that academics are not paid anywhere near as well as their practitioner counterparts.

More importantly, though, I would point to the fact that academia provides a degree of intellectual freedom that being a practicing lawyer simply does not. I don't envy my colleagues working in the UK Foreign Office who have to prepare and present the legal arguments on behalf of the British government, whatever view they may actually hold. I am free to research and critique whatever area or question of international law that I wish, and – ultimately – I can say whatever I think.

James A. Green, Associate Professor in Public International Law,
School of Law, University of Reading

In addition to lecturer/professor type positions, research institutes offer a limited number of employment possibilities for researchers or legal information specialists. Examples include the British Institute of International and Comparative Law (BIICL) and the TMC Asser Institute in the Netherlands.

Let's talk practicalities. Do these jobs pay? How much?

Jobs with international organizations typically pay well. This remuneration may take the form of salary and/or per diems (daily allowances) and even hazard pay in some field postings. UN salaries are tax-free with the exception of a relatively light 'UN tax'. As of January 2014, salaries in professional posts at the UN started at around 46,000 USD, and at the most senior levels approached 189,000 USD (again, for field-based positions there may be a per diem or hazard pay on top of this). Employment with the United Nations also provides benefits, such as re-location grants to assist in moving to your new place of employment and education grants to help with dependent's education.

For organizations such as the OSCE, which rely primarily on secondees, salaries will vary widely between sending states (the British pay quite generously while others pay nothing, leaving their secondees to rely only on per diems). NGO pay varies drastically, from average public sector salaries at some of the larger transnational NGOs (starting salaries with Human Rights Watch and Amnesty International are in the 40-50,000 USD range in London and slightly lower in New York), to 'survival' wages at some of the smaller organizations.

Many positions across the international law field will lack job security. Jobs may be funding-contingent, and in the case of international organizations, depend on the length of and financial support for a particular programme or mission. Once your experience and reputation reach a certain level, however, you are almost assured of having continuous offers of employment. Indeed, the challenge sometimes becomes how to select the offer which is most appropriate. Not to get ahead of ourselves, however, it is important to mention that most people will have to have some period of unpaid or poorly paid work, until they reach a certain level of experience, in order to get the higher level jobs with an international organization or NGO. Aside from internships, early career opportunities may arise through formalised programmes such as the UN's Junior Professional Officer (JPO) programme which offers entry-level positions with one of a number of UN agencies, normally for up to two years. Note, however, that only citizens of sponsoring states are eligible (and in a few cases, applicants from less developed countries). At present, Australia is the only sponsoring Commonwealth state, although the UK and Canada participated until recently and hopefully will again.

Government pay will usually be solid and salaries for legal advisers or legal counsel will often be higher than those within the usual civil service pay structure. University pay structures are usually clearly set out in collectively bargained pay scales, and may be supplemented by the consulting work to which we referred earlier, as well as modest publication royalties. It is difficult to make any generalisations about firms, as remuneration will vary widely depending on size of firm, type of client and legal issue (human rights or petroleum concession agreements?), but generally firms will pay better than other employers.

The bottom line is that doing international law does not require you to resign yourself to a life of poverty. However, it is also safe to say that if you focus on public international law – at least outside the trade and investment arbitration areas – you are unlikely to be earning the same salaries as your colleagues practicing pure corporate and commercial law in the City. You can judge for yourself how important this factor is in your career choice.

> I am aware of the pressures to join particular law firms and the financial incentives attached to such roles. I often hear students talk about the struggle to reconcile law school debts, with a desire to take on (less well paid) public interest work. I certainly don't see these early choices as necessarily exclusive. A legal career may involve many different roles and the expertise you develop is highly transferable to different fields, including within both the public and private sectors.
>
> *Gavin Hood*, Former Legal Advisor,
> UK Foreign and Commonwealth Office, Washington

The most important factor is to find an employer where you will work with other accomplished international lawyers who have an ability both to help you develop skills as a lawyer and also to act as mentors, assisting you to develop your career in the direction you wish.

Antony Crockett, Senior Associate, International Arbitration and Public International Law, Herbert Smith Freehills, Hong Kong

If I decide I don't want to do international law full-time, are there still ways to be involved?

Certainly. Many lawyers choose to work in more 'traditional' areas of domestic legal practice, and to be involved with international law in other, more temporary, ways. We will return to this question in Chapter 3.

2

The Work

What do international lawyers actually do?

There are at least two ways to come at this question. First, we can look at the subject matter of the international law being practiced. Is it climate change or international criminal law? Trade law or the law of the sea? Second, we can look at the type of job. Is it, for example, in 'the field', a courtroom or the headquarters of an international organization?

So what is the subject matter of international lawyers' work?

A quick look at the table of contents of your introductory public international law textbook will give you a sense of the areas of international law within which you could work. Certainly there are commonalities between these areas – they are all public international law and require shared understandings of the nature of international legal processes and the sources of law. Interpreting a treaty or establishing the existence of state practice is the same kind of activity across areas. Having said that, international law is increasingly diverse and specialized (some worry that it has become too compartmentalised in fact) and to say someone is an international lawyer can be about as descriptive as referring to someone as a domestic lawyer. Specializations include: international environmental law, law on the use of force, international humanitarian law, international refugee law, law of international organizations, international criminal law, international trade law, air and space law, law of the sea, law and development and human rights. Some of these categories will have sub-fields of specialization. For example, within human rights you will find specialists on women's rights, children's rights, and torture, among others. Obviously a good many topics can fit under more than one area of specialization. For example, genocide comes within the purview of human rights (the right of a people to survival), international humanitarian law (to the extent that the genocidal acts take place in an armed conflict) and international criminal law (the prosecution of suspected *genocidaires*).

I worked for an ad-hoc international tribunal for six years. During that time, I routinely carried out legal research and analysis on international criminal law, humanitarian law, and human rights. On a weekly or even daily basis, I dealt with the application of the substantive law on genocide, crimes against humanity, and war crimes, as well as the rules of international criminal procedure and evidence.

Alhagi Marong, Legal Affairs Officer, United Nations Mission in South Sudan (UNMISS), Juba, South Sudan

My work involves contact with government representatives to seek to ensure national implementation, often through legislation, of international humanitarian law norms, including the 1949 Geneva Conventions and their Protocols. I provide opinions on both these international obligations, and steps needed to incorporate them into domestic law of the countries I cover. In addition to government contacts, there is also work with National Societies, law professors, the military, NGOs, the judiciary, and international organizations. The work combines both 'pure' international law and comparative domestic law. ICRC Regional Legal Advisers frequently have recourse to our own model laws as well as laws of many other countries around the world to develop legislation for the countries we work in. The areas of IHL covered include the following: incorporating the grave breach provisions of the 1949 Geneva Conventions, working on regulations to ensure proper protection of cultural property in times of armed conflict, working with Parliaments to adopt appropriate legislation incorporating the International Criminal Court Statute, ensuring proper military regulations to prevent the recruitment of child soldiers, and the proper regulation of weapons (such as anti-personnel landmines, cluster munitions, etc).

Christopher Harland, Legal Adviser, Regional Delegation for the United States and Canada, ICRC, Washington, DC

Can I specialize in splendid isolation then?

We want to stress that while specialization is possible, and even desirable for some positions, there are some types of positions you can hold where you will be expected to pick up international law briefs in any number of international law sub-fields. If you are a legal adviser for the Foreign Office for example, you may be asked over the first few years of your career to deal with matters ranging from cyber warfare to 'deportations with assurances' to UN sanctions. Similarly, a legal adviser to an international organization may have to deal not only with the focus of a particular mission or mandate (say establishing a war crimes tribunal) but as well with matters touching on the status of the organization itself. These latter issues can include dealing with the immunities of personnel working for the organization vis à vis the host state and complaints of sexual harassment against an organization or its personnel. All of that said, particularly with NGO work where the organization has a singular focus – say minority rights – it is possible to spend most of your time dealing with a particular subject matter.

Of course, a good lawyer in any field will be able to draw on analogies and parallels from a variety of areas of international and domestic law. Furthermore, skills are transferable across areas and are in many ways more important than the knowledge itself. The latter can always be obtained. Transferable skills include drafting, negotiation, monitoring, advocacy and cross-cultural communication (ideally including facility in a foreign language).

> I predominantly work in international trade law. As this area of international law is inherently not self-contained, I also need to have a solid grounding in other areas of international law including environmental law and human rights. Moreover, the general laws of treaty interpretation and international legal principles are often resorted to in the delivery of the Trade Law Bureau's legal services.
> *Kevin Gray*, Counsel, Trade Law Bureau, Canadian Department of Foreign Affairs, Trade and Development, Ottawa

> My work has predominantly focused on the law on the use of force (*jus ad bellum*), although I have branched out to international nuclear law, the law of cyber warfare and the nature of customary international law. Of course, in terms of teaching, I commonly need to engage with the basic principles of the international legal system (what it is and how it works), although I also get to do a lot of specialist masters-level teaching, both in my main area of the *jus ad bellum* and other key areas of interest (*jus in bello*, international law theory, etc). For the most part, though, you can shape what area(s) of international law you want to engage with as an academic.
> *James A. Green*, Associate Professor in International Law, School of Law, University of Reading

You said there was another way of thinking about what international lawyers actually do?

Yes – think about what practice actually looks like. In the popular – and fair to say legal – imagination, lawyers inhabit boardrooms and courtrooms. That is true for the careers of many international lawyers across all of the specialties mentioned above. International lawyers will work in offices at ministries,

NGOs and international organizations and will wear suits (well, less so in many NGOs where there may be an institutional culture which is less traditional). Similarly, with the explosion in international dispute resolution and international criminal law, lawyers may be carrying litigation bags and may be gowned. However, lawyers may also be deployed to 'the field', as we will discuss in a moment.

> Think carefully not just about what fields of international law interest you most, but also what kinds of work you are most drawn to, such as: advocacy; research work; litigation; legal analysis; legal policy work; legal diplomacy; project management; negotiation or drafting. Sometimes it is the kind of work that can end up being more determinative of your career choices than the specific fields of international law.
>
> *Sarah McCosker*, Legal Adviser,
> International Committee of the Red Cross, Geneva

What kind of jobs can you do with international courts and tribunals?

Two decades ago it would have been almost impossible to have a career as an international criminal lawyer, aside from those working on extradition matters and other forms of cooperation between states. However, as outlined in Chapter 1, the significant rise in the number of international and hybrid criminal courts and tribunals since the early 1990s has meant a massive increase in the number of lawyers employed in international criminal law. Prosecutors, judges and registry officers are employed by all the courts and tribunals. Each judge at the ICC has a law clerk to conduct research for him or her. In addition, although initially neglected, there is now a growing and professionalised international defence bar. Needless to say, there are no entry level positions which will see you in the courtroom at the Hague – indeed there is a political dimension to senior appointments – but there are junior positions in the various court organs which are obtainable by early-career lawyers.

Legal roles in international courts and tribunals vary significantly depending on your job, but two points should be made to distinguish international criminal legal practice from its domestic counterpart. First, lawyers work at the crossroads of a criminal law practice and international law generally. For example, a prosecutor or defence lawyer needs to have traditional advocacy skills and ease with evidentiary matters – usually garnered in a domestic criminal practice – together with knowledge of international criminal law. The second point is that international criminal practice requires intellectual and personal flexibility. Substantive and procedural law, and even courtroom layout, borrow from common and civil law systems (and subsystems) and in this legal fusion or mix we often find a variety of languages requiring interpretation and translation. As well, despite the fact that the two ad hoc tribunals (and, gradually, the ICC) have laid down some key jurisprudence, there are many areas of international criminal law where evolution and change are expected. Playing a role in this evolution – and more importantly, in helping to ensure international criminal justice is done – is undeniably exciting and valuable. At the same time, because international criminal law is a dynamic field, it is not for the intellectually inflexible.

We have focused here on international criminal courts and tribunals but it should be noted that there are dozens of other international courts and tribunals which offer employment in the form of clerkships, administration, case handling and advocacy. The most obvious of these to law students will be the International Court of Justice (ICJ). After years of lobbying by the court, each of the 15 ICJ judges now has their own law clerk who are recruited by the UN as Associate Legal Officers.

> The broad subject matter jurisdiction of the ICJ ensures that the substance of the work before the Court is varied: cases raise questions of, for example, international environmental law, international criminal law, boundary disputes and maritime delimitation, international human rights law, international humanitarian law, etc. The technical skills required are less varied. Although they depend upon the department and team that you are part of, as a general rule, they are predominantly academic and strategic. Some of the key advantages of the job therefore relate to the deep and continuing education in international law and the opportunity to consider often 'novel' and difficult questions of international law. In short, it is a fascinating job.
> *Merryl Lawry-White*, Judicial Assistant/Assistant to the Vice-President, International Court of Justice, The Hague

What about working in the field – what kinds of positions can I find?

One of the most exciting and challenging prospects of an international law career is the possibility of escaping the office and working in the field. As the field dimension is less familiar to law students than the office/courtroom environment, let's spend some time going into what sort of positions are available and what exactly 'in the field' means. Most specialties but not all (such as space law, at least not yet) will have field possibilities. There are three international law branches in particular where field work is common. These are international human rights, international refugee law and international humanitarian law.

Tell me about doing international human rights law in the field?

Doing field work in human rights may involve a variety of tasks but these usually include monitoring. Traditionally this monitoring involves the scrutiny of three different dimensions of state activity: trials; police and prisons. The methods of doing each of these sorts of monitoring are by now well established and are linked to international and domestic human rights standards. For instance, with trial monitoring there are checklists which can be consulted to see whether or not the accused knows the charges against him, has been offered an interpreter where needed, is represented by counsel of her choosing and so forth. Police monitoring may involve interviewing prisoners detained in police stations (torture often occurs at the pre-trial stage where confessions may be forced) and examining police records to determine the time between arrest and taking an accused person before a judge. Prison monitoring will seek to ensure not only that there is no torture, but that the conditions of incarceration meet international and domestic standards (juveniles not mixed with adults, proper records kept, exercise permitted and so on). Where necessary, monitoring of this sort may rely on medical examination and hospital records.

There are also other types of monitoring beyond traditional state monitoring, for example the monitoring of human rights abuses carried out by non-state actors such as insurgents, transnational corporations or private military and security companies. It is fair to say the standard operating procedures in these types of areas are emerging although less well established.

Monitoring results will be compiled and written up into reports which may be released to domestic authorities and international actors for action to be taken. Writing these reports takes specific skills. Reports should carefully assess the evidence, not overstate, and make clear recommendations. Perhaps above all, monitoring and reporting activities must respect the principle of confidentiality of sources of information. Deliberately or negligently released sources of information may result in the death or harassment of that source by authorities or non-state actors. A set of ethical and competency standards have recently been published by the ICRC following consultations with Human Rights Watch, InterAction and other NGOs. *Professional Standards for Protection Work* is available on the ICRC website and should be mandatory reading for anyone embarking on field-centred projects. [http://www.icrc.org/eng/assets/files/other/icrc-002-0999.pdf].

Of course monitoring is not done only for its own sake, though it is important to establish a record of what occurs. Depending on the mandate of the organization, the role of a human rights lawyer in the field may well also extend beyond monitoring into the realm of advocacy. Monitors may make direct representations to police chiefs, prison governors and other authorities. As an example, an ethnic minority group which feels its right to freedom of movement is being unfairly curtailed through restrictive policies on the issuing of passports, or a lack of safe passage through dangerous areas, may ask a human rights lawyer with an IGO or NGO to advocate on its behalf before domestic or international actors. Here, too, diplomatic skills as well as sensitivity to confidential information are crucial. This is an area of international human rights law practice which can be particularly satisfying if the advocacy has its desired effect, though there can be many frustrations – political, logistical and so on – along the way.

What kind of organizations hire human rights field monitors?

Domestic and international human rights NGOs (such as Human Rights Watch, Amnesty International and Minority Rights) hire monitors. So too do international organizations with a field presence such as the OSCE. Monitors may be region or country specific or thematically specialized (eg. torture; freedom of expression; social, economic and cultural rights). Monitoring, reporting and advocacy aside, human rights field work may also involve capacity building with local partners in 'at risk' or conflicted societies. Unlike work with an organization such as Human Rights Watch, this kind of grassroots organising is often carried out by smaller NGOs.

What do international refugee lawyers do in the field?

Much of the work of a refugee lawyer is based on the 1951 *Convention Relating to the Status of Refugees,* the 1999 *Guiding Principles on Internal Displacement,* and several regional instruments, which together provide a template of the basic rights to be enjoyed by refugees and internally displaced persons (IDPs). However, as we have suggested above, a familiarity with other areas of international law, and in particular international human rights standards, is also critical here.

International refugee lawyers undertake a variety of projects, aimed both at governments and individuals. Responsibilities may include the provision of legal assistance and/or advice to refugees and IDPs, or state authorities undertaking legislative reform in the area of refugee protection. Those working under the auspices of the UN (see below) may also be involved with refugee determination cases at the behest of state authorities which do not have the administrative capacity to make those determinations themselves. International refugee lawyers also get involved in legal aspects of 'durable solutions' to displacement – negotiating return to one's home of origin, resettlement in another country, or integration in the community where one has taken refuge. There is also a growing area of refugee law which is concerned with access to justice *within* a refugee camp or other settlement (for example, how are family law or criminal law issues addressed within the camp?).

> When working with UNHCR, the main international law issues encountered surround the signature, ratification and above all, implementation of relevant international conventions by state parties. When states are not signatories to international conventions, UNHCR staff also have to refer to other national or international norms that could apply in the country to ensure refugee protection. A second major legal activity when working with UNHCR is the refugee status determination where both international and legal standards should be applied. Finally, as UNHCR staff you might be in a position to undertake important training or capacity building activities in international law, human rights and refugee law.
>
> What I like the most about working with UNHCR is that the work involves a wide range of activities in the fields of advocacy, technical and operational support. Refugee contexts also vary from one operation to the other (emergency, repatriation, internal displacement, urban refugees, etc.) and there is no monotony in the work. As a Protection Officer, you need to possess a solid legal background but refugee protection also requires that you develop other skills such as negotiation, communication, or simply the ability to show empathy with others. The direct contact with the refugees and being able to impact positively on their protection is one of the most interesting parts of the work.
>
> *Anne Triboulet*, Senior Regional Training Officer (Protection),
> UNHCR Regional Representation, Dakar, Senegal

Who hires international refugee lawyers?

Refugee law is an area which tends to be dealt with by organizations with a fairly narrow refugee law or refugee assistance mandate. In terms of international organizations, the main body is the United Nations High Commissioner for Refugees (UNHCR). UNHCR works in 126 countries with a staff of approximately 7,600 persons. Lawyers with UNHCR will generally work as 'Protection Officers'. With an estimated nine million persons displaced from and within Syria alone in the past four years, these numbers will surely only rise.

The International Organization for Migration (IOM) is also a big actor in this area. An inter-governmental organization with 127 member states and offices in 100 countries, IOM serves both governments and migrants. IOM follows the UN's system of job classification and compensation. Contracts are generally short (up to one year) but, like the UN, once you are in the system you can expect to move fairly easily from one posting to another.

IOM's activities in the field include working with governments on legislative reform in relation to migration, as well as capacity building on migration law with law enforcement officials.

In recent years protection of refugees and IDPs at the UN level has been organised into 'clusters'; under this umbrella other UN agencies such as the United Nations Children's Fund (UNICEF) and the United Nations Human Settlements Programme (UN-HABITAT) are also involved in protection work. Numerous NGOs also specialise in refugee law, many of them with operations in a variety of countries, such as the Norwegian Refugee Council. In some cases these NGOs work under contract to UNHCR to fulfill a particular part of the agency's mandate, such as the provision of legal advice to refugees/IDPs on property issues or return.

> While it can be discouraging to reflect on the number and immensity of the world's problems, it is also a great privilege to be involved in the problem solving. As an intergovernmental organization with a strong operational capacity and an extensive field presence, IOM has given me the opportunity to work with a variety of people, from individual migrants with inspiring stories of vision and courage, to dedicated civil servants and business figures. It has also allowed me to see a lot of the world. An international career can be very hard on families, and there is often limited job security, but it can offer a richness of life experience which is highly motivating.
>
> *Jonathan Martens*, Senior Migrant Assistance Specialist/Head of Unit, International Migration Law Focal Point, Regional Office for Asia and the Pacific, International Organization for Migration (IOM), Bangkok

What does international humanitarian law look like in the field (aside from ducking bullets)?

This is a dynamic and growing field. Increasingly Western militaries deploy uniformed lawyers with their military contingents overseas. The British Army now has legal advisers at the Brigade level, as well as in Headquarters and posted to the Defence Academy. They may advise commanders on matters such as targeting (is this proposed bombing target going to involve harm to civilians in a way which is disproportionate to 'military necessity'?) and the treatment of prisoners. These advisors may also be involved with prosecutions pursuant to a state's international humanitarian law or international criminal law obligations. The latter obligations are set out in the Rome Statute of the International Criminal Court for states which are party to that treaty (at the time of writing 122 states, including the UK, Australia, Canada, Jamaica and New Zealand, were state parties) and the domestic implementing legislation.

The ICRC also has an important field presence and its 'delegates', as they are called, monitor the compliance of belligerents with IHL. These delegates must be able to show the utmost neutrality to ensure the success of their mandate, which involves, among other things, gaining access to the warring parties' prisoner of war camps for the purposes of investigating conditions.

> I work on international law as it touches on civil-military interaction – combining international humanitarian law, human rights, international criminal law, and the law of peacekeeping. I deal with issues such as protection of civilians and the rule of law on a daily basis. I also am called upon to give presentations on the legal framework for civil-military coordination. My previous job was as legal advisor to the International Committee of the Red Cross in Afghanistan. There, I would explore complex issues of IHL and IHRL as they applied to a non-international armed conflict on a daily basis to promote better adherence to IHL by parties to the conflict in Afghanistan. I would advise colleagues of the legal requirements for detention in a conflict and which rights of detainees they should be promoting. I would visit detainees held by international military forces and discuss the conditions of detention with those forces. I would also provide advice on the protection of civilians – recommendations directly to parties to the conflict through written submissions on how they conduct their hostilities, whether they took precautions in attack and whether they have injured or killed civilians, and how not to do so in the future.
>
> *Kelisiana Thynne*, Research Manager, Australian Civil-Military Centre, Queanbeyan, New South Wales

How do I know if I'm suited for a headquarters or field-type position?

One way of thinking about this is whether you want and are willing to tolerate muddy boots or shiny shoes?

As far as international organizations are concerned, working at headquarters can be attractive as it may bring you closer to where the 'big' decisions are made. If you want to have influence on a macro level this may be the environment for you. It may also have advantages for one's personal and family situation, as far as balancing a spouse's professional life or finding good schools for children.

Work in the field – being 'on mission' – will involve logistical challenges such as periods without electricity and hot water, and lack of internet access. Other challenges involve, at times, safety (an area may be mined or one's freedom of movement at night may be limited), a sense of isolation from the centre of decision-making, and challenges to one's personal life. Most definitely there are families which make mission life work but it can be inadvisable (or prohibited by your employer) to bring family members along on some postings, in particular to conflict zones. As working in the field often involves changes of 'field station' as often as every couple of years, there can be big disruptions to accompanying family members' lives, work and education. Women, sexual minorities and individuals with disabilities may face particular challenges depending on the posting.

Work in the field may also raise issues about career progression: there is some concern that going from the field to a headquarters position is more difficult than vice versa. On the other hand, in the field, you are at the 'coal face' of international law dealing with the real and immediate problems of vulnerable individuals. You also may have significantly more autonomy than you would in an office environment (your supervisor may be hundreds of miles away). Finally, having some field experience will give you a sort of credibility which 'HQ' people who have never been in the field will not have. This 'edge' can serve you well even if you ultimately do transfer to a headquarters-type position. At the end of the day, making these decisions will be a matter of personal preferences, values and qualities, and, of course, job availability.

Working in the field with an organization such as UNHCR might have an impact on family life. UNHCR is present in many remote or non-family locations. Staff posted there are separated from their families for some time and often have to adapt to very basic living and working conditions. However, while frequent travels can have disadvantages, the rotation system in place within UNHCR, by which staff members are obliged regularly to change their duty stations, also offers the possibility to settle for a certain amount of time in very diverse parts of the world which is most of the time a very enriching experience.

Anne Triboulet, Senior Regional Training Officer (Protection),
UNHCR Regional Representation, Dakar, Senegal

I like the fact that my work is intellectually stimulating and challenging and the range of tasks is very diverse. What can be frustrating is that you sometimes feel that you are not making a difference (ie nothing would have changed if you were not doing your work). I imagine this is particularly true so for those who work in headquarters, rather than the field.

Sergey Ripinsky, Legal Affairs Officer, International Investment
Agreements (IIA) Section, UNCTAD, Geneva

There is an incredible amount of variety in the work that I do – both in terms of thematic areas and geographic focus. One day I may be working with colleagues on land access issues around a site in Africa, the rights of indigenous peoples in Australia or labour rights relating to a supplier in Asia. It is great also to be able to work with people who are at our sites as

well as the corporate office. I am also fortunate to be able to contribute to
the policy discourse in this area. The role can be very busy with quite a bit
of travel so it's necessary to stay committed to a work/life balance as much
as possible.

Vanessa Zimmerman, Human Rights and Business Specialist,
Resource Sector

**This all sounds interesting but I'm still not sure if international law is
for me – how should I decide?**

Working in international law in most capacities can be exciting and provides
a real sense of job satisfaction. You have the potential, after all, to promote
the rule of law in international affairs and, in some areas, have a very real and
direct impact on peoples' lives. The three main reasons people give as their
motivation for going to law school – intellectual challenge, pursuit of social
justice and a good standard of living – can all be fulfilled in an international
law career in a way that might not be possible for some personalities in, say,
a corporate-commercial law firm environment. Every dimension of international law has its drawbacks however. Let's take working for an international
organization as an example. Working either in HQ or in the field you will
almost certainly face mind-numbing bureaucratic inefficiencies and you may
well face other depressing facts such as political expediencies trumping sound
policy or discrimination in the workplace. Furthermore, as leading international law scholar Martti Koskenniemi and others have noted, international
law is not inevitably progressive: the language of human rights has been used
to justify aggressive wars for example. In sum, it is important not to over-
romanticise international law careers.

I wish the pace of work at the ad-hoc international criminal tribunals had
been faster. With hindsight, one realizes that some of the trials went on for
far too long. It is hoped that this is one of the lessons that the
International Criminal Court would learn from the work of the ad-hoc
tribunals, in addition to the rich body of law that has emerged from almost
two decades of administering international criminal justice.

Alhagi Marong, Legal Affairs Officer, United Nations Mission in South
Sudan (UNMISS), Juba, South Sudan

One drawback of private practice is that opportunities to influence policy-
making are more limited than they are with other employers, for example,
in government, or with an NGO. By its nature, private practice is also
limited by the matters and cases which come through the door.

Miranda Rushton, Senior Associate, Carter-Ruck Solicitors, London

The disadvantages of working for the government include lower salaries, lower professional profile (we do not have our photos and CVs featured on websites) and, in eras of budgetary restraint, less frequent opportunities for advancement. Furthermore, bureaucratic processes intended to ensure government transparency, fairness and public accountability can slow down decision-making and reduce flexibility of action. In contrast, private law firms are more nimble and can adapt to changing circumstances quickly. Government lawyers have to learn to live within a more rigid framework and adapt accordingly.

> *Mark Luz*, Counsel and Acting Deputy Director, Trade Law
> Bureau, Canadian Department of Foreign Affairs,
> Trade and Development, Ottawa

How will you know if international law is right for you or what particular type of work is for you? The place to start is with an honest self-assessment of your values, goals, strengths and weaknesses. If you don't enjoy travel and cross-cultural exchange for starters, you are thinking about the wrong career. If you are lucky enough to have access to a careers advisor who know something about international law careers (they are a rare species) then that is obviously a good starting point as well. Next, do as much reading as you can on international law careers (aside from this book, the American Society of International Law and American Bar Association-International Law Section each put out careers guides which should be consulted, though they are both US-focused) and start speaking to international law academics and practitioners. Meet the latter at conferences and try to develop informal mentoring links as part of a wider network (discussed in the next chapter). However, it may not be until you actually do an internship or get some other sort of 'job shadowing' experience that you will know for sure.

3

Getting Hired

Any general words of advice on getting an international law job?

As you will have noticed, law firms with a corporate-commercial focus put out glossy brochures and the path to employment is laid out; not to say that it is an easy path, of course, but it is clearly laid out. The path to a successful career in international public law, on the other hand, often requires creativity, flexibility and, to use an old-fashioned word, gumption. International law posts are more clearly advertised than they were 15 or 20 years ago (when more than a few people obtained jobs 'in theatre' by showing up in Sarajevo or Arusha and simply knocking on doors) but it is still fair to say that pursuing international law careers is not for the faint-hearted. Now, if we did not think that these jobs were obtainable, we would not have written this Guide, so keep reading.

Practically speaking, what do I need to do? What should I do in university for starters?

 You need a 'good' degree in law (marks do matter, but that certainly isn't the end of the story). In much of the Commonwealth this is an LLB, though some schools (including most Canadian common-law schools) are rebranding their LLBs as JDs. In the UK, the conversion course to law is also an option, although this route leaves very few possibilities to take international law courses. Some people come to international law careers without an undergraduate law degree but with a degree or work experience in a related discipline like international relations. Most of them will supplement their degree with a Masters in international law, since some law schools offer law Masters to non-law graduates.

While in law school you should take as many international law courses as possible. Every school 'worth its salt' will offer a basic course in public international law. Some schools are even starting to make this course mandatory – or at least a fusion course like transnational law (which teaches both public and private international law and the amorphous 'law and globalization'). Common options which may be available at your school include international human rights, international criminal law and international trade law. In the UK, European Union (EU) law is mandatory but in other Commonwealth law schools this course may be offered as an option. As the EU becomes increasingly active as an international law actor, taking this course can be useful even for law students outside the EU. Less common are courses in topics such as international humanitarian law and the law of the sea, and some specializations, like air and space law, are very rare. In these specialized areas of the law, Masters courses are available and are considered the baseline for advancing in the field. To stick with the air and space example, most students will pursue a Masters in the subject at McGill University, Leiden University, or a handful of other schools. We'll return to Masters courses in a moment.

In universities where there are few options beyond the basic Public International Law course – or if you simply have a burning desire to go deeper in a particular area of the law – consider taking a supervised writing credit in international law. Approach professors or lecturers who might act as supervisors early and with some tentative research behind you. Finally, if your school is lacking in international possibilities, seriously consider an exchange, studying elsewhere on a 'letter of permission' or even transferring to a university with a more solid international law programme.

Aside from international law courses, also take any comparative law courses you can find. For example, if your law school offers a course on the civil law, take it. Substantive and procedural international law draws on both the common and civil law traditions; since common law graduates are typically ignorant of the civil law approach and vice versa (and this ignorance leads to missteps in practice more often than is generally perceived) even a cursory understanding of the civil law will give you a leg up. Some universities will also offer courses in Islamic Law, among other comparative subjects, and some offer joint degree programmes with universities in other countries. For example, Essex University offers a joint LLB-Licence en Droit with a partner university in France and the University of Windsor in Canada offers a Canadian-American dual-degree programme with a partner school in the US. At least one law school, the Faculty of Law at McGill University in Montreal, offers a transsystemic (common law/civil law) approach to law throughout its curriculum, and the European Law School at Maastricht University in the Netherlands offers an English-language Bachelor of Laws programme which includes training in the common law and civil law as well as international and EU law.

Savour the opportunity to study now, because the vast array and tempo of legal issues in international practice leaves little time for calm academic study and reflection.

Gavin Hood, Former Legal Advisor, UK Foreign and
Commonwealth Office, Washington

What about activities outside of the classroom at law school?

Do an exchange if financial and personal circumstances allow. All law schools offer exchanges; don't miss the opportunity, particularly if the host school is one operating in a civil law system. Not only will it relieve the tedium of law school and give you new intellectual perspectives, but you will show potential employers that you have cross-cultural experience under your belt. Several European exchange partners – notably in the Benelux and Nordic countries – offer courses in English for exchange students, but if you have or are developing a second language, consider studying in that language.

If you don't have at least a second language already, start working on getting one. There are unilingual anglophones who have successful international law careers, but you definitely have an advantage if you have at least a functional knowledge of a second language, particularly if that second language is one of international or regional importance such as French, Russian, Arabic and Spanish. Even a less widely-spoken language will be useful, so draw upon your heritage languages if you have any. Your school may even allow you to take a language course for credit. While of course fluency is nice, strive for at least functional competency in your second language.

Get involved with your law school's international law activities. Join clubs with an international law focus. If your school doesn't have an international law society, start one. In Canada, for example, NGOs such as the Canadian Lawyers' Association for International Human Rights (CLAIHR) and Canadian Lawyers Abroad (CLA) have chapters in many law schools. There may also be relevant clubs in your wider university such as an Amnesty International or United Nations Association chapter. Also, don't think only in terms of your particular university or even country. Organizations such as the European Law Students Association (ELSA) or the International Law Students Association (ILSA) offer excellent opportunities to get involved in international law. If you do join a club, be prepared to work hard and bring something to the table by showing leadership on a particular initiative. The reward will be experience, greater knowledge and an expanded network (we will return to this network in a moment), as well as the satisfaction of contributing to international civil society.

You might also work on an international or transnational law journal or seek a part-time research position with a professor who engages in international law research (offer to do the research on a voluntary basis if necessary). Finally, many students find mooting to be a favourite activity at law school, and participation in a moot can help students hone advocacy skills and deepen their legal knowledge. You will also gain contacts among the participants, coaches and judges and, through this, begin developing your international network. The Jessup Moot competition is the leading international law moot, and hypothetical problems raise several international law issues for argument. Law schools worldwide participate in this moot. Other moots are on specific topics, such as the Jean-Pictet Moot on International Humanitarian Law, the Lachs Space Law Moot and the ELSA WTO moot. Some competitions are restricted to teams from certain countries or regions, such as the European Telders International Criminal Law Moot, the Canada-US Niagara Moot and the Australian Red Cross International Humanitarian Law Moot.

Any advice for the summer vacations?

Our advice on this is very clear: if you can possibly afford to, do an internship or volunteer during the holidays with an organization doing international law work. At the very least, try and get a brief 'job shadowing' opportunity. As we will come back to in a moment, there are virtually no international law jobs for which you will be hired directly out of your LLB/JD. These jobs require experience, which most people get through internships and volunteering. So, start as early as you can by building an international law profile and expanding your network. An increasing number of law schools offer logistic and financial support for summer activities, with participants competitively selected.

> I would suggest that law students undertake as many internships as they can. They will gain inside knowledge and observe the functioning and real work of specific organizations. If students target the United Nations, I also suggest they undertake internships both in headquarters and in the field so that they can make an informed decision on whether or not they are prepared to work in the field.
> *Anne Triboulet*, Senior Regional Training Officer (Protection), UNHCR Regional Representation, Dakar, Senegal

Whether volunteering at an NGO, doing a placement at a tax law firm or flipping burgers, you might also – time and money permitting – think about short courses in international law which you can take in the summer. Notable in this regard is the Hague Academy's summer programme in international law – with instruction by some of the 'heavy hitters' in the field – but there are many others including online, some of which are referred to in Appendix B. Some law schools offer academic credit for accredited study abroad programmes.

After law school? Do I need a Masters? If so, where and in what subject?

There are no set rules on this. Our advice is that you need at least a Masters degree *or* a professional qualification (your 'ticket' as a barrister or solicitor). Ideally you would have both. There are many practicing international lawyers who have one or the other, and very few who have neither.

A Masters can deepen your knowledge in a particular area or areas of law. Several factors will go into determining where to do your Masters, including specialities and programmes, reputation, presence of scholars you would like to work with, whether you want to do the Masters at home or abroad (we recommend the latter if feasible) and funding (even if you don't think your undergraduate marks are stellar, ask/apply for scholarships all the same). In addition, we are not unmindful of the fact that many students are interested in how law schools are ranked. We are skeptical about rankings generally, especially as schools are often not ranked on international law alone.

All of the top law schools provide excellent LLM opportunities in international law, but cautions are in order. First, the emphasis of each school will be different and students should undertake detailed research to determine what programme is right for them. Second, there are many other excellent institutions falling lower in the rankings, which, depending on your particular interests, cannot be excluded from any sort of 'top places to do an LLM' in the UK. So, use the rankings as only one criterion in your search. In the US, too, a great deal of attention is paid to rankings by law students and law school administrators. The most widely cited general ranking is that of the US News and World Report, which includes both a general ranking as well as a specifically international law-focused one.

In terms of the subject matter of a Masters programme, don't feel unduly pressured to 'put all your eggs in one basket' as far as subject matter is concerned. Many Masters programmes will allow you to take taught courses at the beginning and then choose to write a thesis on a particular question towards the end of your degree, when you will have a better idea about what it is that actually interests you. If at all possible, seek to have your dissertation published (of course you will have to adapt it for publication) in an academic or practitioner's journal. Publication can serve to establish you as an expert in a particular field and is demonstrable proof of research and writing skills. In terms of a starting point as to where to submit your paper, have a look at the journals which you have cited in your own writing, though do be aware that the most prestigious law journals will be very competitive. Needless to say, disseminating your work need not happen exclusively through law journal articles. Blogging, tweeting and posting on online repositories (notably SSRN) are good ways to get your ideas – and name – out there.

My advice to any lawyer considering a career in international law, is do not sell yourself short by specialising too soon and focusing on too narrow an area. Instead, get a good first degree in law, followed by an LLM in public international law; in the process try not to overspecialise. For those considering entering the practice of international law, including working for a government or an international organisation, a good understanding of treaty law or dispute settlement can provide an invaluable starting point.

Mary Footer, Professor of International Economic Law,
University of Nottingham

Some people may be curious about doctorates. If you are interested in an international law career as an academic, then you must seriously consider a PhD; increasingly, professors or lecturers hired throughout the Commonwealth either have a PhD or are completing one. We use the term PhD here as it is most common in the UK, but other designations for a doctorate in law, depending on the university, are DCL, DPhil, LLD or SJD (not to be confused with the American JD or Juris Doctor which is actually a first degree in law). Doing a PhD is not to be undertaken lightly – the process can be gruelling and long – though the intellectual rewards can be great. If you are interested in practice and not academia, you may be just as well to focus on building your career with the Masters as the highest degree you need, but opinion on this varies. Certainly if you want to do a PhD and practice in the field of international law, be sure to choose a cutting edge topic and focus on publishing the results of your research as you go.

Get as much experience as possible, as early as possible. To get an academic job in international law you must now have a PhD, and that's a huge commitment to take on. So, during your degree, see if you can do any research assistant work or get involved in some other way with research work going on in your department. There are always opportunities to act as a research assistant for international lawyers in your school (sometimes paid, sometimes unpaid). It's the best way to find out if the career is really for you, and also looks great on the CV later down the road (even if you end up doing something completely different).

James A. Green, Associate Professor in International Law,
School of Law, University of Reading

How necessary is becoming a barrister or solicitor if I don't want to practice domestically?

As we said above, you generally need to have either a Masters or a professional qualification (and preferably both) to be taken seriously in the job market. Whether you become a barrister or a solicitor is not very important.

Indeed the question is irrelevant in parts of the Commonwealth where there is a fused profession. And some people choose to get admitted in certain states of the US, notably New York, where you can simply write the bar exams without attending a legal practice/bar vocational course. At a minimum, having a professional qualification gives you a state-sanctioned credential that you are legally trained, have no serious criminal record and are subject to an ethical code. Rightly or wrongly a professional qualification gives you a degree of credibility with potential employers. It also gives you the possibility of practicing domestically and building your legal skills while you search for international work, a process which can take some time (see our note on 'keeping your hand in' at the end of this chapter).

Of course if you intend to have a career in international law litigation, then you must have a professional qualification as a bare minimum. In what is probably near the top end of required experience, for example, the International Criminal Court requires defence counsel to have at least ten years of relevant practice experience. Other tribunals have less stringent requirements; theoretically anyone selected by a state can appear on its behalf before the International Court of Justice.

You've mentioned internships a couple of times; what can they do for me?

Internships give you experience and contacts. Some of that experience will be in photocopying, so accept that, but you will also get a chance to see what international law looks like in at least one of its guises (an NGO, court, etc.). You will have a chance to see if it is for you. You should establish the nature of the internship as clearly as possible from the start and ensure that it is properly designed. Look for an opportunity that will provide you with relevant, hands-on experience, such as doing research and drafting legal documents, and the possibility of shadowing your principal. If you can find a mentor at the organization you are working for, the potential exists to have a truly rewarding experience. You will also be contributing to an organization and programme in international law (and you really have to have a positive attitude of 'what can I contribute today' for an internship to be useful for you and your host organization).

Most internships pay nothing; some pay a small stipend or expenses. In some countries, including across much of the Commonwealth, there is increasing resistance to the "tyranny of the internship" as an exploitative form of extracting unpaid labour from recent graduates. While this may eventually result in changes to the role which internships play in career development, for the moment at least it remains the way things work for large swathes of international law practice. Our best advice is to carefully consider the potential career benefits to you, and to make sure that working conditions are clearly agreed upon, before signing on.

The summers while in law school are good opportunities for three month internships. Likewise, if you can manage it financially, an internship following graduation can provide you with a more extended experience with a host organization and the chance to really contribute to its work.

Speaking in purely careerist terms for a moment, an internship will give you an important line on your CV that counts as experience towards paying jobs. Perhaps most importantly, as we have said, you will begin to build a mutually supportive network. You will need this network to tell you about advertised and unadvertised job opportunities, to 'put in a good word for you' with potential employers, to offer you advice as you approach a new task or area of the law, to give you contacts with local interlocutors in field positions, and the list goes on. Obviously this is a two-way street, so you should be thinking about how you can support the people in your network.

> Working in the international human rights field often means working for free, at least initially. While it may be frustrating to be unpaid, and there may not immediately be a job on the horizon, look at unpaid internships as an important opportunity to showcase your skills and make a good impression. The human rights community is small; demonstrating a strong work ethic, careful research skills and a solid writing ability will serve you well in the future. At Human Rights Watch we have a large number of interns every year, but those that worked hard and really took the internship seriously stand out. Almost all of those interns now have good jobs – in part because we were able to strongly recommend them.
> *Param-Preet Singh*, Senior Counsel, International Justice Program,
> Human Rights Watch, New York

> I completed an internship with the United Nations Office of Legal Affairs prior to commencing work with Clifford Chance. This was a very useful experience as it gave me insight into the role of the United Nations in developing international law. My short time at the UN has also helped me to build and maintain a professional network beyond the private sector.
> *Antony Crockett*, Senior Associate, International Arbitration and
> Public International Law, Herbert Smith Freehills, Hong Kong

In some circumstances it is possible that a post-graduation internship may lead directly into paid employment with the organization. If it seems appropriate, let your interest in working with the organization be known. However, also be aware that some organizations, including most UN agencies, make former interns ineligible for paid positions for a period of at least six months following an internship, so do keep thinking about your next steps while you're in the internship.

How do I get an internship?

Some law schools have established links with employers to offer internships to their students. If yours does not, consider (perhaps through your international law club – there is strength in numbers) asking your careers advisory service to set one up. Outside of formal law school programmes there are increasing numbers of internships which are clearly advertised, and we provide an indicative list in Appendix A. Be creative here. If you want to work with a particular organization, practitioner or firm, contact them and see if you can set something up. Be sure to indicate how you can contribute by doing your research and proposing an interesting project. Have your CV highlight your international law experience and interest – even if this is only through things you have done at law school it will count more than your months behind the cash register before law school. Some employers have become inundated with internship requests, but starting early, and showing perseverance and flexibility, will pay off for you in this regard.

You mentioned that internships are normally unpaid or poorly paid; is there any way to get financial help with my expenses?

In a word, yes – but again, be prepared to do some legwork. Start with your law school; even if there is no formal internship programme there may either full or partial funding available for those who arrange their own placement. Also check for government or other funded internship programmes, either with established internship links or with funding for self-organised ones. For example, the Canadian International Development Agency (CIDA) runs the International Youth Internship Programme which offers hundreds of international internships, many of them law-related, to Canadian graduates under 30 years old. There are also a few schemes around which provide funding to law students undertaking self-arranged fellowships or internships. For example, Helton Fellowships of the American Society of International Law offers 'micro-grants' to more than ten students per year. Students from any country are eligible to apply. The Australian and New Zealand Society of International Law (ANZSIL) has a similar programme for permanent residents of those two countries undertaking internships with international organizations. The Human Rights Lawyers Association in the UK offers bursaries for individuals who would otherwise be unable to afford to take an unpaid internship.

Once you have pursued these avenues, and if more funding is still required, start writing letters and working the phones. Contact any organization or business that might have an interest in the work you plan to do during your internship – service or diaspora community groups, religious organizations and companies who do business in the region where you are planning to go, for example. Also contact your country's embassy or high commission in the country or region where you are going and ask if they would be prepared to fund part of your internship – they may have human rights or rule of law programme funding, for example, into which your work could fit. With a little perseverance, you will in all likelihood end up with *some* funding, but not enough to cover all your expenses. Again keeping in mind what we mentioned above about the controversy over unpaid internships, all we can say here is that even if you have to go into extra student debt to allow you the opportunity of an internship, you are not likely to regret it in the long run.

I have some internship experience; now how do I get a proper job?

As mentioned above, you may be hired by the organization with which you interned, sometimes after a mandatory gap period. Otherwise your search will have to broaden. Hopefully by this point you've started to get an idea of what subject and what work environment you are most interested in, and have built up the beginnings of a profile in these areas.

> Target the employers that will offer you the best possible training as a lawyer. Employers that offer the opportunity to rotate through various practice areas and have a strong ethic of training young lawyers are the best places to start your career. Whereas you will have the opportunity to shift the focus of your practice and move to different employers, you only have one chance to start your career under the tutelage of great practitioners. Subject-area specialization is less important at the beginning of your career. For example, even if you know you want to practice international arbitration, if you can find a law firm or government ministry that will give you the chance to spend some time doing project finance or corporate securities, take that opportunity. Even if you know you want to do international human rights law for an NGO over the long-term, spend a couple of years doing commercial litigation with a barrister willing to train you to be an effective advocate. The first two years of your law career are crucial. Good habits of writing, attention to detail, client-relations, strategy and analysis of legal and factual issues have to be developed early on and there is no better way to do that than working somewhere that takes training of young lawyers seriously.
>
> *Mark Luz*, Counsel and Acting Deputy Director, Trade Law
> Bureau, Canadian Department of Foreign Affairs,
> Trade and Development, Ottawa

There is a lot of variety among potential employers, and so it helps to have a clear idea of how one wants to be of service, but also how flexible one is prepared to be when it comes to what one does and where. Some organizations concentrate their officials in New York or Geneva for longer periods of time to better support the drafting and negotiation processes of the principal UN bodies. Other organizations disperse their officials more broadly around the world to engage more directly with people in need, national governments, local NGOs or businesses, or to assist in places where state authority is weak or where it has collapsed. In my career with IOM, I've been able to work in Africa, Europe, and now Asia. The diversity has required me to be flexible, and to contribute according to needs as they arise. While international law and the international system are an ever-present backdrop, I have spent much more of my time on strategic planning, policy development, project development, operations, and management than I ever would have expected when I was in law school.

Jonathan Martens, Senior Migrant Assistance Specialist/
Head of Unit, International Migration Law Focal Point,
Regional Office for Asia and the Pacific,
International Organization for Migration (IOM), Bangkok

Unfortunately there is no one or even several places to point you to, to ensure that you receive notice of all the jobs with international organizations or NGOs. The list of employers in Appendix A is a place to start; more generally go to the websites of any organizations you are interested in. There are also 'clearing houses' for international law jobs. One of the main ones for UN and other international organization work is UN Jobs [http://www.unjobs. org]. When looking for jobs, be realistic about what you are qualified for. Normally you will be applying at the entry 'program officer' level rather than at the 'coordinator' level (though the nomenclature varies). Your network will be important to you in this job search. Keep your CV up to date and be sure to tailor it and your cover letter to the particular employer you are approaching. Also, if you are interested in UN jobs, keep your United Nations Personal History Form (P11) up to date.

Wherever possible put your name forward with agencies that are on the lookout for qualified experts. In the UK, for example, register with Electoral Reform International Services (ERIS) if you are interested in election and democratization postings. Some countries have NGOs or QANGOs which act as centralized databases for international law experts. In fact, Canada's CANADEM accepts qualified applicants of all nationalities for its roster of individuals looking for employment with UN agencies, multilateral organizations, national governments and NGOs. It will contact you when it finds international law jobs for which you may be qualified. It will also forward your CV and application to potential employers.

Some UN agencies also keep their own rosters of qualified potential employees. UNHCR for example has established an International Professional Roster of potential entry-level officers; to apply to be put on the roster you must have an LLB/JD and four years' relevant experience, or a Masters or PhD and two years' experience. The bottom line is that you need to get your name out wherever you can at this point. Getting the first international law job really is the hardest, and from there others should follow. We have seen eminently qualified lawyers apply for dozens of jobs over the course of a year before it all came together, so have confidence – it will work out if you are diligent. Also be aware that the bureaucratic wheels of international organizations can move *extremely* slowly. It may be months after applying before you receive an interview and a further delay before hearing whether you have the job (though, ironically, when the offer comes you may be required to go within a few short weeks).

> Remember about patience and perseverance – it can be really difficult to break through. It was for me, when I applied probably to 35 law firms for my first internship, and got rejections from 34. I was almost desperate, but then my last chance worked out. My feeling is that after you get your first international experience (scholarship, award, etc.), and perform well, things tend to get easier.
>
> *Sergey Ripinsky,* Legal Affairs Officer, International
> Investment Agreements (IIA) Section, UNCTAD, Geneva

If you are hoping to join a government agency in your own country, again go to the relevant webpage and check the information posted there. Here too there is often intense competition and the process may be long. While you are still in law school, start checking into what qualifications are necessary for these positions. You should also look into whether there are any additional hurdles to cross, such as sitting a diplomatic service exam to work in your foreign office as a legal adviser (this is not necessary in the UK but is in many other Commonwealth countries).

As for careers in academia, this too can take time and competition is intense. Apply for every position which looks mildly related to your field of interest. To be frank, if you have expertise or experience in any other field of law you may find you need to apply on that basis as well (tort lawyers may be in higher demand than international lawyers since the subject is mandatory). You can always gear your research in the direction you want to go once you are appointed, and over time you can probably find some balance in teaching between international and the traditional 'core' subjects. Again though, the number of international law posts at universities in the UK and the rest of the Commonwealth should only continue to grow as international law continues to become seen as a core area of the curriculum.

The bottom line, of course, is that the qualifications required or sought after will depend on the employer and area of international law. Here are comments from a few of our contributors about what they or their employers look for:

International firms will expect all applicants to have an excellent academic record (i.e. first class or upper second class honours). A postgraduate degree in public international law is not essential but in my opinion it can be very valuable as it demonstrates a keen interest in the subject. In the field of international dispute resolution it is increasingly rare to encounter lawyers without a postgraduate degree. Language skills are also extremely valuable.

Antony Crockett, Senior Associate, International Arbitration and Public International Law, Herbert Smith Freehills, Hong Kong

In an international Prosecutor's Office, in general, the qualifications and skills required reflect the different functions to be performed. Investigating, presenting evidence in court, examining witnesses, drafting pleadings, researching and advising on substantive or procedural law, establishing and maintaining diplomatic relations, tracking fugitives and reviewing and disclosing evidence are the type of tasks involved.

The cases dealt with are usually large and complex, involve a range of witnesses from victims to experts, include many different types of evidence from highly technical to basic fact evidence, can be document heavy and relate to a foreign context. There is no single domestic legal job or experience that comes to mind that is the exact equivalent. Though there are some types of legal practice which may be closer to the work of an international criminal prosecutor, such as large scale white collar crime or organized crime cases, relevant experience can come from a variety of jobs. The type of legal work that develops analytical skills, attention to detail, document management, teamwork, litigation skills, researching and drafting and time management will provide the key building blocks for working on international criminal cases.

Norman Farrell, Prosecutor, Special Tribunal for Lebanon, The Hague

In my experience strong candidates for a position as a Government international law adviser would need to be qualified lawyers, with very good academic qualifications, including at least a Masters degree in international law, which gives a very strong grounding in the fundamentals of international law. Ideal candidates would also have: work experience as a lawyer, preferably with experience in the interpretation and application of international law; excellent written and oral communication skills; the ability to analyse and synthesise large volumes of complex material; the ability to get across new areas of law and policy well; very good time management and project management skills; the ability to work well in small teams but also to work independently. Governments also tend to seek people who are adaptable and resilient, able to work and deliver results in a fast-paced environment; and presentable and capable of representing their department effectively and diplomatically in engagement with diverse Government and non-Government stakeholders.

> *Sarah McCosker*, Legal Adviser, International Committee of the
> Red Cross, Geneva (Formerly Principal Legal Officer, Office
> of International Law, Attorney-General's Department,
> Australian Government, Canberra)

Vacancy notices can be quite long and detailed, but I think the most important qualities for UN positions are the following:

– Enthusiasm about, and knowledge in, the field of law that you are going to be working in. The former is obligatory, while the level of the latter can depend on the seniority of the position. Post-graduate qualification (e.g. specialized LLM) is a useful indication although, it is not seen as an automatic proof of the above qualities.
– Ability to speak fluently in the working language of the organization (English in my case).
– Ability to draft in correct English, in a structured, logical, precise and concise manner.
– Intellectual curiosity, willingness and ability to learn continuously, initiative and creativity (as opposed to automatic following of instructions), striving to always work to the maximum of your capability, sense of responsibility for the work product (these qualities are difficult to assess at the interviews, but they can be easily judged during the probation period).
– Friendly personality (a person hiring you should feel that you can get along with him/her and the rest of the team).

> *Sergey Ripinsky*, Legal Affairs Officer, International Investment
> Agreements (IIA) Section, UNCTAD, Geneva

As an employer I look for a good education first. Basic knowledge of law, or related fields, and some skills in research and computers. That said I look more deeply for honesty of purpose, a disposition that is open, integrity and a willingness to learn and contribute. I am really looking for character then one can pour in one's own experiences and guidance. It is a delight to see skills improve, confidence grow and contribution increase. Sometimes though one is disappointed at the selfishness with which the environment is used and the sense of privilege and entitlement that is exhibited.

Maja Daruwala, Director, Commonwealth Human Rights Initiative, New Delhi

Fellows and interns will need outstanding academic records, completed law degree, fluency in English and/or French, with specialization in international dispute resolution or public international law an asset. Examples of experience that our fellows and interns have had: research assistant to professors or arbitrators; interns at other international organizations; summer associateships at law firms; and Jessup or Vis moot or law journal at university. Sometimes, depending on the case load, specific languages are sought after, for example we recently recruited Russian and Portuguese lawyers based partly on their language skills and cases on our docket which are conducted in those languages.

Legal counsel will need to be admitted to practice law in their home jurisdiction with several years of work experience, preferably in arbitration or public international law at a law firm or an arbitral institution. Ideal candidates will have excellent communication, organizational and interpersonal skills. Examples of experience that our legal counsel have: global law firm (practising arbitration, litigation and/or commercial law); clerking for judges in national courts; internships at other international organizations, tribunals or arbitral institutions; working for a national government; teaching at university; and most have LLMs or PhDs.

Judith Levine, Legal Counsel, Permanent Court of Arbitration, The Hague

I've just started my domestic legal practice; how can I keep my 'hand in' international law?

As mentioned above, the first thing to note is that international law has in many ways entered the 'mainstream' in domestic legal practice, so that the question of domestic or international law is no longer a binary one. The reception of international law in domestic law raises exciting issues and arises in a variety of cases, from matters of national importance such as those highlighted by the Pinochet litigation and claims brought against militaries for actions overseas, to matters of personal importance such as immigration and adoption. Unfortunately too many lawyers practicing domestically still lack the training to spot issues where international law is relevant and can be used to the benefit of their clients. Some forward-thinking law schools have begun sensitizing students to the transnational dimensions of private practice, but this is not yet widespread.

You may also wish to build up international experience within the context of a domestic legal practice as a stepping stone to a more exclusively international legal career. It's never too late. Indeed you will have been building up lawyering skills which will make you useful to whatever organization you approach. Be sure to highlight these transferable skills in your cover letters and CVs. Especially in some areas – notably international criminal law – extensive experience in private practice is a real asset.

There is a good deal of public international law work at the Bar, but most of it is firmly rooted in the soil of domestic law. To succeed, a practising international lawyer needs first and foremost to be a good lawyer: the international expertise is almost useless without a knowledge of domestic law and basic lawyering skills.

Vaughan Lowe QC, Barrister, Essex Court Chambers;
Emeritus Professor of Public International Law,
Emeritus Fellow of All Souls College, Oxford University

Do not be disappointed if a job in international human rights does not work out right after law school! I try to encourage law students to get experience domestically after law school – whether it is in a law firm or government, for example – to develop strong research, writing and advocacy skills that can be used in the international human rights field. The skills taught in law school are a good foundation, but international organizations are more interested in how those skills have been applied in the 'real world' in recruiting candidates.

In choosing a job after law school, think long-term about where you want to be: for instance, if you eventually want to be doing international criminal law, getting solid experience as a criminal lawyer domestically will be invaluable later on. If you are interested in refugee work (like working for UNHCR, for instance), consider doing immigration work at home.

Param-Preet Singh, Senior Counsel, International Justice Program,
Human Rights Watch, New York

Don't be set on an international law job from the beginning – it is unlikely to happen straightaway. Do internships, take a general government or NGO job, but continue to volunteer in areas that interest you – a local charity, environmental group or your national Red Cross/Red Crescent. It is all valuable experience and you'll be contributing meaningfully to the practical application of international law.

Kelisiana Thynne, Research Manager, Australian Civil-Military Centre,
Queanbeyan, New South Wales

Good junior lawyers are a key asset to any Prosecutor's Office as they, for example, conduct legal and factual research, prepare evidence summaries, assist in the disclosure of evidence, draft memoranda, and generally assist in much of the preparatory work for trial or appeal. Yet, lawyers who wish to start their legal career by working in the field of international criminal law have to be mindful of the implications of the choices they make. For example, in cases of this nature it is difficult to find opportunities for inexperienced lawyers to get courtroom exposure and to progressively develop in court. Unlike domestic jurisdictions where a litigator may over time be able to gain experience starting with less serious cases, the international tribunals are not the place to progressively develop courtroom advocacy skills. Though there are exceptions, it is unlikely that the necessary advocacy skills needed to be promoted to a more senior trial counsel position will be obtained.

If it is the goal of a new lawyer to become a skilled courtroom advocate, it may be wiser initially to develop those skills in their national jurisdiction.

Norman Farrell, Prosecutor, Special Tribunal for Lebanon,
The Hague

For those considering a career in international law, it appears valuable, from what I have seen, to qualify first in one or more domestic jurisdictions. Qualifying as a lawyer shows commitment, but more importantly, it assists to understand the principles, philosophies, institutions, etc. present in a legal system. It is also develops an appreciation for how international law may play out in practice. An intensive few years focused on developing skills required as a lawyer also seems to be an important stepping stone (as, of course, the start of a long process!). I was lucky enough to spend several years learning from exceptional (and patient) lawyers in an international law firm.

Merryl Lawry-White, Legal Assistant/Assistant to the Vice-President,
International Court of Justice, The Hague

In your domestic-oriented practice experience you should also be able to demonstrate interest and experience in international law through activities such as publishing, and active membership in international law organizations such as BIICL or the International Law Association (ILA), which has branches at the country level (some more active than others – the British branch is a particularly active one) and conference attendance. The annual conferences of the ILA-British Branch, the Australian and New Zealand Society of International Law, the Canadian Council on International Law, the Indian Society of International Law and the American Society of International Law all provide useful venues to keep current and connected, as do BIICL, Chatham House and various law school events. Also, stay informed – and be prepared for opportunities and interviews – by following current events and following some key list serves or blogs on international law topics. If you have to choose one list serve, it should be the American Society of International Law's *Insights* and if one blog then the European Journal of International Law's 'EJIL:Talk!' Some lawyers also successfully use an LLM in an international law subject as a way of transitioning into more internationally-focussed work after some years of domestic practice (see our discussion above of LLM programmes).

Some lawyers whose practices are exclusively domestic in nature may satisfy their international law inclinations through periodic 'infusions'. You may do this through *pro bono* international legal work. Others may do international legal consulting on the side, or may take a leave of absence of several months or a year from their ongoing employment to work with an international organization or NGO. Elections monitoring is one way to keep your hand in international law while still maintaining a domestic legal practice. Organizations such as ODIHR, mentioned in Chapter 1, send both short-term (about ten day missions) and long-term (about three months) monitors to emerging democracies to monitor the fairness of elections processes. Britain and Canada, among others, regularly send monitors to participate in these missions. Short-term monitors are generally not paid but receive generous expense coverage, while long-term monitors will normally receive a per diem.

Lawyers wishing to pursue international law work while primarily practicing domestic law within the private sector are increasingly able to do so. Certain areas of private practice afford lawyers the necessary expertise and economic stability to pursue cases involving international human rights or international criminal law, which are often pursued on a *pro bono* basis. For instance, a practice concentrating on plaintiff side tort litigation will lend itself nicely to holding accountable a foreign sovereign for *jus cogens* violations or multinational corporations complicit in international crimes abroad.

The provision of legal services to various international organizations can also be pursued alongside a litigation practice. For instance, as trial observers for the International Bar Association's Human Rights Institute, lawyers attend select hearings worldwide in order to ensure that the right to a fair and public trial is being observed.

Following my work experience abroad assisting the Constitutional Litigation Unit of the Legal Resources Centre in their representation of families of deceased mineworkers at the Marikana Commission of Inquiry, and as a trial observer in Zimbabwe, I have returned to domestic practice, alongside which I am involved in the American Bar Association's Business and Human Rights project.

Sandra Wisner, Barrister & Solicitor, Litigation Practice,
BL Law, Toronto

Can you give me some real-life examples of international lawyers' career paths?

Yes. Here are the career paths of four of our panellists – one relatively recently established in international law, one mid-career and two senior international lawyers. As you can see, they do not necessarily follow straight lines.

> I read law at university and trained as a solicitor at a City firm in London. On qualification I spent a year in the banking department, before moving firms to specialise in commercial and insurance litigation. I was several years qualified when I decided to change practice areas to international law. I started by studying for an LLM in Public International Law at University College London. After that I carried out internships at the British Institute of International and Comparative Law in London, the International Institute of Humanitarian Law in San Remo, and the UN International Criminal Tribunal for the former Yugoslavia in The Hague. I went back into private practice two years ago when I joined the international law team at Carter-Ruck in London.
>
> *Miranda Rushton*, Senior Associate, Carter-Ruck Solicitors, London

> I did my undergraduate law degree alongside an arts degree in Australia. Before commencing work as a commercial lawyer I was able to undertake several human rights related internships in Geneva including at the Office of the High Commissioner for Human Rights. While training as a commercial lawyer and as my career developed it was important to me to continue working in the human rights area including through *pro bono* work. I then decided to take the leap and look for a specific human rights role but knew from my internships that a strong post-graduate degree in international human rights would be a great asset. I completed an LLM focusing on human rights at Harvard and then was lucky to find a role supporting the UN Special Representative of the Secretary-General on Business and Human Rights, Professor John Ruggie. After Professor Ruggie's mandate finished I began some consulting work for a variety of stakeholders and was delighted to consult for and then join a major extractives company as its group human rights advisor.
>
> *Vanessa Zimmerman*, Business and Human Rights Specialist, Resource Sector

> I did my first law degree at the University of New South Wales in Australia, followed by a masters at NYU. I returned to Australia to do some teaching and worked for a judge of the High Court of Australia, and then spent a year as an adviser to the Australian Attorney-General. An

opportunity arose for recent NYU law graduates to apply for judges' assistant positions at the International Court of Justice, which was my first exposure to life as an international lawyer in The Hague. I worked mostly with Judge Rosalyn Higgins on a variety of cases before the ICJ as well as helping her with research projects. After that, I was ready to practice law. I knew I wanted to return to New York, yet still do some public international law, so I went to White & Case, which had a practice group renowned for representing sovereign clients. I spent five years there doing a mix of public and private arbitration, some litigation and a good dose of *pro bono* work, before returning to the Peace Palace, this time to work at the Permanent Court of Arbitration (PCA). At the time, the PCA was experiencing an increase in cases with a perfect blend of public and private interests which seemed to match my experience and interests. There were 17 PCA-administered cases when I arrived in 2008, and now there are 96, so it's been an exciting period of growth. While at the PCA I have had the opportunity to work on some big cases, including serving as Registrar or tribunal secretary on the Abyei Arbitration between the Government of Sudan and the Sudanese People's Liberation Movement/Army, the Philippines v. China dispute over the South China Sea and the recently concluded Yukos arbitrations which resulted in the Russian Federation being liable for 50 billion dollars under the Energy Charter Treaty. In 2011-12 I was posted to the PCA's Mauritius office where I helped promote Mauritius as a place for dispute resolution, particularly in the burgeoning area of Asia and Africa related disputes, and undertook capacity building projects with the local judiciary, university and legal profession.

Judith Levine, Legal Counsel, Permanent Court of Arbitration,
The Hague

I was practising law in a community in Montreal when I decided to pursue postgraduate studies essentially out of intellectual interest and with no particular career ambitions. After completing an LLM, I continued with a doctorate, in international law, and this opened the door to a new career for me. I started teaching at university but was assigned to teach subjects other than international law. However, working with NGOs provided opportunities for travel and I soon became a 'player' in international human rights law and international criminal law circles (including sitting on the Sierra Leone Truth and Reconciliation Commission).

William Schabas, Professor, School of Law, Middlesex
University, London, Honorary Chairman of the Irish Centre for
Human Rights at the National University of Ireland,
Galway and Head, United Nations Human Rights Council
Inquiry Commission into Gaza

Any final words of advice?

Public international law offers numerous, viable career options and should not be seen as an 'alternative' career. That said, a career in this area will not likely fall into your lap. Be focused and start step-by-step research and portfolio building. The following appendices, which deal with short courses, Masters programmes and internships should help in this regard. At the end of the day, though, both luck – favouring the prepared – and trial and error have roles to play.

Appendix A

Internships

There are literally hundreds of established internship options. Any attempt at a comprehensive listing of available internships would shortly be outdated (the most up-to-date information will be found on the organizations' websites). We highlight a few here simply to illustrate the depth and variety of internships available. Internships are grouped into three categories: international organizations, courts, and NGOs.

1. International organizations

African Union Commission
http://www.africa-union.org/root/UA/Emploi/AU_Internship_Policy.htm

The African Union Commission offers internships for university graduates. Internships are unpaid and are offered for up to three months on a rolling basis. Applicants are requested to apply three months ahead of the date they wish to take up an internship, and to indicate in what area of the Commission's work they are interested.

Council of Europe
http://www.coe.int/t/jobs/traineeship_en.asp

The Council of Europe (CoE) offers traineeships to allow students the opportunity to learn about the organization's structure, activities and international cooperation. Trainees undertake research and draft reports and studies for experts' meetings as well as drafting meeting minutes. Along with other CoE institutions, four sections of the European Court of Human Rights (ECtHR) offer traineeships: Legal Divisions; Case-Law Information and Publications; the Just Satisfaction Division; and the Research Division. Candidates must normally be nationals of one of the CoE's 47 member states, and selection is made according to the principle of fair geographic distribution. Applicants must speak one of the CoE's official languages (French and English) fluently and knowledge of the other language is preferable.

Traineeships with the Council of Europe are unpaid and run for three month periods (January to March, April to June, and September to

December). The application deadline for all three internship sessions is normally in September of the previous year. Applicants to one of the ECtHR divisions must have an undergraduate degree in law and knowledge of human rights issues, in particular the *European Convention on Human Rights*.

European Commission
http://ec.europa.eu/stages/index_en.htm

There are around 1300 traineeships with the European Commission each year. Traineeships with other EU institutions such as the European Court of Justice should also be considered. Each trainee is supervised by an advisor through the traineeship.

Traineeships begin in March or October (application deadlines are in September and February respectively) and last either three or five months. Trainees receive a monthly stipend of 1000 Euros as well as travel expenses between their permanent address and their place of appointment. Applicants must be university graduates.

Organization of American States
http://www.oas.org/EN/PINFO/HR/gen_information.htm

The Organization of American States (OAS) Student Intern Program is designed for senior undergraduate and post-graduate students to allow them to work within their fields of study, while acquiring knowledge of the organization.

Internships with the OAS are unpaid. To be eligible, applicants must have good university results and a good command of two of the four official languages of the OAS (English, French, Portuguese and Spanish). Applications for the two and a half month summer session are normally due in the preceding November.

Organization for Security and Co-operation in Europe
http://www.osce.org/employment/91

The Organization for Security and Cooperation in Europe (OSCE) offers a limited number of internships in its offices in Vienna and Prague, as well as with its field missions in Eastern Europe and the former Soviet Union.

Internships with the OSCE are unpaid and usually last between two and six months. To be eligible applicants must be in their final year of university at the undergraduate or post-graduate level, or be recent graduates. The upper age limit for interns is 30 years (oddly, age discrimination is not uncommon in international organizations). Applicants should also have a working knowledge of oral and written English, and computer literacy.

Internship applications should be received at least three months in advance of the envisaged period of internship.

United Nations
http://www.un.org/Depts/OHRM/sds/internsh/index.htm

UN Headquarters in New York offers internship opportunities to students currently enrolled in a post-graduate programme. These internships are located at the offices of the UN Secretariat, and are designed to provide an operational framework through which post-graduate students may be exposed to the work of the United Nations, while providing UN offices with student assistance.

Internships with the UN Secretariat are unpaid. Application deadlines normally fall approximately three months before the beginning of the relevant internship session. All applications must be made through the United Nations Human Resources website ('Galaxy'), which can be found at the link above.

New York HQ is far from the end of the story on UN internships, however. A vast number of UN agencies also have internship programmes. UN peacekeeping missions may also accept interns; check the websites of the individual missions.

For those with an interest in international trade law, it is worth making specific mention of internship possibilities with the International Trade Law Division (ITLD) of the UN Office of Legal Affairs (http://www.uncitral.org/uncitral/en/vacancies_internships.html).

World Trade Organization
http://www.wto.org/english/thewto_e/vacan_e/intern_e.htm

The World Trade Organization (WTO) Internship Programme provides a limited number of internships for university graduates who have completed at least one year of post-graduate study. Internships are geared towards students who wish to gain practical experience and deeper knowledge of the multilateral trading system, and of trade policy more generally. Applicants must be nationals of a WTO member state or a country engaged in WTO membership negotiations.

Interns with the WTO receive a daily allowance of CHF 60 (approximately £37). Intake to the Programme is on a rolling basis; a roster of qualifying candidates is maintained. Internships can start at any time of the year and generally last for up to 24 weeks, although the length of the internships will vary according to the project and the needs of each Division. Interns must be between 21 and 30 years of age. All internships are based in Geneva.

2. Courts

International Court of Justice
http://www.icj-cij.org/registry/index.php?p1=2&p2=5&p3=4

The International Court of Justice (ICJ) offers one- to three-month internships for students and young professionals. Interns are placed in all departments and divisions of the Registry. Applicants should be fluent in English and French.

   ICJ interns are unpaid. Applications are accepted on a rolling basis and are submitted via the ICJ website. Applications are kept on file for eight months.

International Criminal Court
http://www.icc-cpi.int/en_menus/icc/recruitment/Pages/recruitment.aspx

The International Criminal Court's Internships and Visiting Professionals Programme offers internships to 'highly motivated young professionals with good academic qualifications who are in the early stages of their careers.' Interns assist the staff of the Court in discharging their duties, and are assigned projects and tasks relevant to their educational background and interests. The Court offers internship opportunities within each of its three organs: the Presidency and Chambers; Office of the Prosecutor; and Registry.

   Internships are offered for three to six months, and each organ sets its own recruitment deadlines. To be eligible, applicants must hold a degree or be in the final stages of their university studies and must be under 35 years of age. Applicants should have a background in one or more of the following subjects: national and international criminal law; public international law; international humanitarian law; human rights law; comparative law; and criminology. Additionally, applicants must have good oral communication and drafting skills in one of the working languages of the Court (English or French); and knowledge of any other official languages of the Court (Arabic, Chinese, Russian and Spanish) is considered an asset.

Ad-hoc international criminal tribunals
http://www.icty.org/sid/113
http://www.unictr.org/tabid/122/default.aspx

The International Criminal Tribunals for Rwanda (ICTR) and the former Yugoslavia (ICTY) have been excellent training grounds for young international criminal lawyers in recent years, with scores of law students and recent graduates having undertaken internships with the Tribunals. These opportunities are still available and details are provided here; however interested students should act soon as the Tribunals are slated for closure. Other mixed international/domestic tribunals, such as the Special Court for Sierra Leone or the Special Tribunal for Lebanon, should also be considered.

The ICTR Internship Programme is geared towards providing offices at the ICTR with the assistance of students and professionals specializing in fields relevant to the work of the Tribunal. The Programme is offered to individuals who are currently at least enrolled in a post-graduate programme, and internship opportunities are available at the offices of the ICTR in Arusha (Tanzania), Kigali (Rwanda) or The Hague (the Netherlands). ICTR internships are unpaid, and are available for a period of two to six months. The programme does not consist of clearly defined internship positions; rather, the ICTR will define the number and nature of internships, on a continuous basis, according to the needs of the various offices.

The ICTY offers 'regular' internships with each of the three constituent organs of the Tribunal: the Registry, Chambers and the Office of the Prosecutor (OTP). All regular internships with the ICTY are unpaid, and are of three to six months' duration. Applicants are advised to submit their applications six months ahead of their preferred start date. Although a legal education is not a prerequisite for many of the internships within the Registry, most of the available opportunities within the Chambers and OTP do require applicants to be in the upper or final year of their law studies. The OTP also offers a 'restricted' internship, which is a shorter, two to three month commitment and is open to students not yet in the final stages of their law studies.

3. Non-Governmental Organizations

Amnesty International
https://careers.amnesty.org/

Amnesty International is an NGO focused on respect for internationally-recognised human rights. The organization regularly accepts interns from around the world at its International Secretariat offices in London, Geneva and New York. Internships with Amnesty are unpaid, although interns in London are eligible for small subsidies for daily travel and meals. National offices of Amnesty also offer internships. For example Amnesty International Canada offers internships in its office in Ottawa, and Amnesty International Australia hosts interns in its Melbourne office.

Positions are advertised on a rolling basis and decisions made within roughly six weeks of the application deadline. These internships generally run for four to six months. Responsibilities include research and media monitoring. Positions in national offices may have specific deadlines and run from three to six months.

British Institute of International and Comparative Law
http://www.biicl.org/internships/

Located in London, the British Institute of International and Comparative Law (BIICL) offers internships to students who have recently completed an LLM or are enrolled in a post-graduate research degree in law. Internships can be in a variety of areas including public international law, private international law and EU law. Strong research and/or drafting skills are required and a background in international or comparative law is preferred. Interns assist with research on current applied research projects, research for the development of new projects and the organisation of events (among other things).

Internships can be undertaken on a part-time basis – for around three days per week for a period of three to four months – or on a full-time basis over a shorter period. Internships with the BIICL are unpaid. There are rolling deadlines for internships.

Center for Constitutional Rights
http://ccrjustice.org/jobs

A US-based non-profit organization, the Center for Constitutional Rights (CCR) offers opportunities for law students to assist CCR lawyers with their case load while taking part in educational seminars and talks. Students work with a team of lawyers, undertaking legal and factual research on active cases and research projects involving international human rights issues, among others.

The CCR annually offers two funded fellowships for law students under the Ella Baker Summer Fellowship Program (each valued at $3,500). The CCR may also be able to offer other funding for law students unable to secure funding on their own. Internship application deadlines for ten-week summer internships are in November for first-year law students and in January for second-year students.

European Council on Refugees and Exiles
http://www.ecre.org/about/this-is-ecre/vacancies.html

The European Council of Refugees and Exiles' (ECRE) internship programme, based at the organization's Brussels office, is designed to give students a grounding in immigration and refugee issues. Responsibilities include research, analysis and monitoring of refugee policy and human rights law in the European context. Most interns are given the opportunity to participate in one external meeting or training session during their internship.

ECRE internships are unpaid although a small contribution towards travel within Brussels by public transport is provided, as are lunches. Internships last six months. Application guidelines are posted on the organization's website when a position becomes available. There are normally about 5 interns working in the Brussels office at one time. Applicants should have proven knowledge of and interest in international and European asylum as well as human rights issues as they pertain to refugees, and a good knowledge of the EU institutions. Applicants should hold at least an undergraduate degree, be fluent in English and ideally another European language. Applicants must be eligible to live in the EU.

Foundation for International Environmental Law and Development

http://www.field.org.uk/get-involved

The Foundation for International Environmental Law (FIELD) is based in London and accepts interns from around the world. Its staff are public international lawyers whose work encompasses campaigning, research and traditional legal representation (often *pro bono*). Interns assist with research, drafting position papers and editing academic papers.

Law school graduates and those in the final year of a law degree may be considered for an internship with FIELD, however preference is given to post-graduate applicants or those with relevant experience. Internships are unpaid although some assistance with transportation expenses within London may be available to those in financial need. There are three intake periods for interns each year, with application deadlines several months ahead of the potential start date.

Human Rights Watch

http://www.hrw.org/about/volunteering

Human Rights Watch, a leading human rights monitoring NGO, accepts interns in its London and New York offices as well as other locations. Placements are available in sections including Advocacy and International Justice, as well as in sections with a specific geographic focus.

Human Rights Watch interns are unpaid. Internships are generally offered for three to four months and may be full- or part-time. Both current law students and recent graduates are eligible to apply. Students should have a strong interest in international human rights and/or criminal law, and possess strong writing skills. Application deadlines are rolling.

International Crisis Group

http://www.crisisgroup.org/home/index.cfm?id=1154&l=1

International Crisis Group (ICG) is an independent, non-profit, non-governmental organization that works through field-based analysis and high-level advocacy to prevent and resolve deadly conflict. ICG offers internships at their Brussels, London, Nairobi, New York City and Washington offices. Each office offers a variety of different internship opportunities.

ICG internships are unpaid and normally last anywhere from three to six months (with the possibility of a one-year renewal). These internships are geared towards current undergraduates, recent graduates and post-graduate students. Application requirements vary from office to office. Though not strictly speaking legal positions, these internships provide an opportunity to contribute to analysis of conflicts incorporating norms of public international law, international human rights law, and international humanitarian law.

International Environmental Law Research Centre
http://www.ielrc.org/about_careers.htm

The International Environmental Law Research Centre (IELRC) is an independent, not-for-profit organization, established in 1995, with offices in Geneva, New Delhi and Nairobi. It undertakes policy-related research on environmental legal issues from a North-South perspective. Interns are accepted in one of the three offices for at least one month and work primarily as research assistants. Internships are unpaid; applications are reviewed on a rolling basis.

International Organization for Migration
http://www.iom.int/cms/en/sites/iom/home/about-iom-1/recruitment/internships-at-iom.html

The International Organization for Migration (IOM) offers internships to students to facilitate their learning about the organization's activities, gain initial work experience, and (if applicable) prepare for a degree dissertation in an area related to IOM's work. In addition, IOM explicitly states that interns will be evaluated for their suitability for future employment contracts. Interns are assigned a supervisor for the duration of the internship. At any given time there are between ten and 15 interns working with the organization.

IOM grants Geneva headquarters-based interns a monthly subsistence allowance, although this will be insufficient to cover all living expenses. Internships last between eight weeks and six months. Application is on a rolling basis; for Geneva internships application should be made via the e-recruitment section of the IOM website, and for internships in field missions applicants should e-mail directly the mission in question.

Redress

http://www.redress.org/employment–internships/opportunities

Redress is a London-based human rights organization working for justice and reparations for torture survivors. It offers legal internships to recent law graduates and LLM students. Legal interns work on individual cases and background research for larger files.

Interns are unpaid and work at least two full days per week for a minimum of three months. Application deadlines are rolling. Students should have a strong background in public international law, human rights and international development law and strong research skills. Knowledge of foreign languages, in particular Spanish, Arabic, Russian and French, is particularly desirable.

Finally it is worth noting that sometimes the best internships are not advertised but rather created by or at the request of an individual applicant. If you know on what topic you would like to work, and/or in what geographic region, research the organizations in that area and contact ones you feel might make good hosts. There is a good chance they will be happy to have the free assistance.

Appendix B

Short Courses

Short courses provide exposure to, and intensive training in, a particular area of international law. They also provide an opportunity to make contacts with teaching staff and fellow students working in these areas. Further, they can be taken in 'down time' such as summer vacations or before or after internships while you are doing your job search. They are also a way of receiving some overseas education even if you are unable to pay for graduate studies abroad. In some cases it may also be possible to receive credit towards your law degree by completing these programmes – check with the administrators of the programme you are interested in as well as with your home university. Likewise, Continuing Professional Development/Continuing Legal Education credit may be available for the purposes of your law society/bar obligations. In most cases accommodation is available, either at an extra cost or provided as part of the registration fee. Unless otherwise indicated, the language of instruction of all courses listed here is English. For the most part courses are grouped geographically, however, thematic links between courses offered in different regions are also drawn. Some online courses are also noted; although these do not provide the same networking and pedagogical benefits, they are useful where money or time is short.

1. United Kingdom

International Law in Practice
British Institute of International and Comparative Law
http://www.biicl.org/events

International Law in Practice is a four-day programme run by the British Institute of International and Comparative Law in London, which provides a broad introduction to key issues in international and comparative law – from public to private and from commercial to human rights. It has been offered twice annually, in April and September, since 2013.

Led by many of the Institute's leading researchers and practitioners, the course is ideal for those in the early years of legal practice, those working in governmental and NGOs with legal elements to their work, and students who are about to commence a postgraduate degree in aspects of international law.

International Human Rights Law Summer School
Oxford University, New College
http://humanrightslaw.conted.ox.ac.uk/SSIHRL/

The International Human Rights Law Summer School, established in 1995, runs for four weeks yearly (mid-July to mid-August) at New College, Oxford. Course offerings cover a variety of aspects of international human rights law including practice, history, philosophy and doctrine. Law students, lawyers, and others working in fields related to international human rights are eligible to apply. The course offers streams of study both for those seeking an introduction to international human rights as well as those seeking to deepen their knowledge and skills.

International Human Rights Law Short Course
University of Nottingham Human Rights Law Centre
http://www.nottingham.ac.uk/law/hrlc/courses/

Nottingham's Human Rights Law Centre (HRLC) has offered its International Human Rights Law Short Course twice annually since 1997. The three-month courses run from October to December and January to March. Prior completion of an undergraduate law degree is recommended but not essential. All students take a general course on International Human Rights Law as well as three to four courses from Nottingham's LLM course offerings on related topics. Short course students also have the opportunity to participate in seminars and workshops at the HRLC during their stay.

In recent years the HRLC has also offered other programmes including a summer course on children's rights.

International Summer School in Forced Migration
Oxford University Refugee Studies Centre
http://www.rsc.ox.ac.uk/

This interdisciplinary Summer School has been held annually since 1989 and runs for 3 weeks in June. It is geared towards academics and graduate students, practitioners and policymakers. The course addresses legal, political and social issues surrounding forced migration. Large-group, small-group and individual work is expected, with the goal to foster a culture of the 'reflective practitioner'.

York University's Refugee Studies Centre also offers a Summer Course on Refugee and Forced Migration Studies in Toronto, as does the Institute International des Droits de L'Homme in Strasbourg (in French).

International Law: Contemporary Issues
London School of Economics (LSE)
http://www.lse.ac.uk/collections/summerSchool/courses/Default.htm

LSE offers a course in International Law as part of its larger annual summer school. The course runs for three weeks in July and August.

Summer Course in EU Law
King's College London
https://www.kcl.ac.uk/prospectus/shortcourses/index/name/eulaw/keyword/summer-school

The Summer Course in EU Law is a ten-day programme on selected topics in EU Law including the external relations of the EU. Instruction is provided primarily by King's College Faculty.

2. Europe

Summer Schools on the International Criminal Court and Minority Rights
Irish Centre for Human Rights, National University of Ireland, Galway
http://www.nuigalway.ie/human_rights/summer_schools.html

The Centre offers two week-long workshops in international law, the subjects of which are the International Criminal Court (ICC) and Minority Rights. The ICC course is well respected and is taught by a panel of experts, several of whom have had direct involvement with the Court since its inception.

Paris Summer Institute in International and Comparative Law
Cornell University Law School
http://www.lawschool.cornell.edu/international/study_abroad/paris_summer

Cornell University and the Université Paris I Panthéon-Sorbonne jointly offer a five-week academic programme in international and comparative law held annually in Paris. Courses offered vary from year to year but topics of interest to budding international lawyers may include international human rights, international criminal law and international commercial arbitration. The course is open to students who have completed at least one year of law school and law graduates from around the world.

There are many other courses of this type coordinated by American law schools and held outside of the US, some of which, like this one, accept non-US law students. A good starting point is the website of the International Law Students Association, which lists more than 100 such courses:
http://www.ilsa.org/listing/study-abroad-programs

Summer Courses in Public and Private International Law
Hague Academy of International Law
http://www.hagueacademy.nl/

The Hague Academy offers the 'gold standard' of short programmes in international law. The courses run in July and August annually, with each course lasting three weeks. Classes are held in both French and English; those given in French have simultaneous English translation available. Students may register for one or both courses in a particular year. Students who already have a high level of international law expertise may apply to sit difficult exams at the end of each session to receive the prestigious Diploma awarded by the Academy.

Summer Course on Space Law and Policy
European Centre for Space Law
http://www.esa.int/SPECIALS/ECSL/SEM9YSGHZTD_0.html

The Summer Course runs for two weeks in late August/early September and is hosted by a different European university each year. Lectures are given by university lecturers and 'space professionals'. Topics covered include space-related treaties and UN resolutions, as well as other legal issues concerning space including telecommunications, intellectual property rights, and the commercialisation of space activity. Undergraduate and post-graduate students in law, as well as law graduates, are eligible to apply. The programme is more reasonably priced than most summer programmes – the tuition of 200 Euros for Europeans (800 for others) includes accommodation – and some travel costs may be offset.

Basic Course in International Human Rights
Danish Institute for Human Rights
http://www.humanrightscourses.dk

Courses at the Danish Institute for Human Rights run year-round on a varying schedule. The Basic Course in International Human Rights runs for two weeks. The course is aimed primarily at practitioners working with NGOs, state institutions and international organizations with operations in developing countries, countries in transition to democracy and post-conflict countries. It seeks to provide participants with a basic understanding of international human rights principles and to provide networking opportunities for individuals working in this sphere. The Institute also offers a variety of other short courses with international legal aspects.

Summer Course on International Humanitarian Law
International Institute of Humanitarian Law
http://www.iihl.org/site/5442/default.aspx

This two-week course is held in June and July, and is split between San Remo, Italy (on the Mediterranean coast near the French border) and Geneva. During the Geneva portion of the course students meet with officials and experts of the UN Office in Geneva and the International Committee of the Red Cross (ICRC).

Bilingual Summer School on International Criminal Law
Grotius Centre for International Legal Studies/TMC Asser Instituut
http://www.grotiuscentre.org/SummerSchoolInternationalCriminalLaw.aspx

Held in The Hague, the city which hosts the ICC and ICJ (for starters), this two-week course in June and July is open to law graduates and upper-year students. It addresses both substantive and procedural aspects of international criminal law.

Teaching Session on International and Comparative Human Rights Law
International Institute of Human Rights
http://www.iidh.org/actualite-57-44th-annual-study-session-in-international-and-comparative-law-of-human-rights.html

This three-week course of the International Institute of Human Rights (IIDH), held in Strasbourg, is centred each year around a different theme in international human rights law. The session is large, accepting 400 students from more than 100 countries. Like the Hague Academy, the IIDH also offers students already possessing extensive knowledge of international and comparative human rights law (including a completed post-graduate degree) the possibility of sitting for exams for a Diploma. Some competency in French is required.

3. Commonwealth

Peace Operations Training Courses
http://www.kaiptc.org/Training.aspx

The Kofi Annan International Peacekeeping Training Centre in Ghana offers courses for military and civilian participants on various aspects of peace operations. Several of the courses have legal dimensions.

There are other peacekeeping training centres worldwide, including Canada's Pearson Centre. The Peace Operations Training Institute (POTI) offers a number of online peace operations courses: http://www.peaceop-straining.org/.

Professional Short Course on the Law of the Sea
Australian National Centre for Ocean Resources and Security
http://ancors.uow.edu.au/shortcourses/index.html

The short course on the Law of the Sea is held over five days. Lectures are given primarily by Faculty of the University of Wollongong.

Also consider the Rhodes Academy of Oceans Law and Policy, jointly run by European and American university partners and held in Rhodes, Greece.

Short Courses in Good Governance
University of Pretoria Centre for Human Rights
http://www.ggp.up.ac.za/

The Good Governance Programme at South Africa's University of Pretoria offers a series of week long courses throughout the year including International Law, International Humanitarian Law, Development and Human Rights and International Criminal Prosecutions.

Summer Course in International Humanitarian Law
University of Ottawa Human Rights Research and Education Centre
http://www.cdp-hrc.uottawa.ca/?page_id=84

This one week course, co-sponsored by the Canadian Red Cross and the International Committee of the Red Cross (ICRC), runs annually in June in Ottawa. Canadian citizens and permanent residents are eligible to participate.

In cooperation with the ICRC, other national committees of the Red Cross offer similar programmes. For example the Polish Red Cross (in English) and the French and Belgian Red Cross Committees (in French) regularly offer courses; the British Red Cross occasionally offers a course as well.

4. Rest of World and Online

Short Courses in International Governance
United Nations University (UNU)
http://unu.edu

The United Nations University (UNU) System comprises the UNU Centre in Tokyo and a worldwide network of Research and Training Centres and

Programmes assisted by numerous associated and cooperating institutions. The UNU International Courses are organized annually for postgraduate students and professionals wishing to pursue international careers, including with the United Nations, multinational corporations, NGOs and national foreign service organizations.

Courses offered include Governance of Emerging Global Issues; Environmental Change: Globalization and the Multilateral System; and International Trade and Development. All UNU International Courses take place in Japan, although see the UNU website for courses offered at other research centres.

Summer Programme in International Law
Xiamen Academy
http://www.xiamenacademy.org/introduction

The Summer Programme, held in Xiamen, China, was established in 2005. It is geared to young academics, diplomats, officials of international organizations and other related professionals from around the world. The three-week programme takes place in July of each year. Lecturers are experts in international law from a variety of foreign universities.

Summer Workshop on International Organization Studies
Academic Council on the United Nations System/American Society of International Law
http://acuns.org/programsan/acunsasils

This two-week course has been held annually since 1991 and is geared toward lawyers, academics and practitioners working with NGOs and international organizations in the early stages of their careers. Location varies: in recent years the Workshop has been held at universities in Austria, the United States, Canada, Belgium, Slovenia and India.

United Nations Intensive Summer Study Programme
John C. Whitehead School of Diplomacy and International Relations, Seaton Hall University/United Nations Association of the USA
http://www.unausa.org/programs/john-c-whitehead-school-alliance/un-study-program

This one week intensive course, held on the campus of Seton Hall University and at UN Headquarters in New York, offers an introduction to the inner workings of the UN. Seminars are led by UN officials, as well as representatives of governments and civil society. The course is open to undergraduate and post-graduate students and university credit is available.

A number of short courses focussed more exclusively on international law are also offered on campus by American law schools. American University Washington College of Law's Academy on Human Rights and Humanitarian Law, and Columbia University's Summer Program in International Human Rights, are two examples.

UPEACE Institute
University for Peace (UPEACE)
http://upeace.org/academic/spec_programmes/institute/index.cfm

Headquartered in Costa Rica, the University for Peace was established in December 1980 as a Treaty Organization by the UN General Assembly. To ensure academic freedom, the University was established under its own Charter, approved by the General Assembly. The University's programme is innovative and multicultural and reflects the peace and security objectives of the United Nations. The UPEACE Institute consists of one to three-week short courses on subjects which include the environment, peace, conflict, terrorism, development and food security. Courses run in January annually.

Specialised Human Rights Institute
Human Rights Education Association
http://www.hrea.org/index.php?base_id=275

This offers a wide variety of online courses of various lengths – some as short as three hours – on diverse human rights issues (from rights of the child to EU migration law and policy). HREA also runs an annual class-based Advocacy Institute geared towards staff members of NGOs and inter-governmental organizations with a mandate related to human rights.

International Criminal Law MOOC
http://www.mooc-list.com/course/introduction-international-criminal-law-coursera

The MOOC (Massive Open Online Courses) phenomenon is coming to international law, with a free international criminal law course taught by leading expert Michael Scharf, launched in 2013.

Appendix C

Masters Programmes

This appendix focuses on taught, English-language Masters programmes, though many of the Universities listed below also offer research LLMs. It is intended as a browser's guide and the list is indicative only. As in Appendix B, for the most part courses are grouped geographically; however thematic links between courses offered by universities in different regions are drawn. Comprehensive, country by country and university by university guides can be found at http://www.llm-guide.com. The criteria you may wish to consider in selecting a Masters course are outlined in Chapter 3.

1. United Kingdom

London School of Economics, University of Oxford, University of Cambridge, University College London
http://www.lse.ac.uk/collections/law/programmes/llm/llm-prospective-b.htm
http://www.llm-guide.com/university/118/university-of-oxford-faculty-of-law
http://www.law.cam.ac.uk/courses/llm.php
http://www.laws.ucl.ac.uk/study/graduate/llm-programme/

The London School of Economics (LSE) offers an LLM in Public International Law covering a broad array of subject areas. Oxford, Cambridge and University College London all have 'blue-chip' Public International Law programmes as well.

University of Essex
http://www.essex.ac.uk/coursefinder/course_details.aspx?course=LLM+M10112

The 'grandfather' of human rights Masters programmes, graduates are found in just about every international human rights field mission going.

University of Nottingham
http://www.nottingham.ac.uk/law2/postgrad-taught/index.php

With its deep international law faculty base, Nottingham is able to offer a wide array of modules across the subdisciplines of PIL, including international criminal law. Its respected Human Rights Law Centre should also be mentioned.

University of Reading
http://www.reading.ac.uk/law/pg-taught/law-pgt-courses.asp

Reading offers an interdisciplinary Masters degree in International Law and World Order, with courses offered in both international law and international relations.

There are many other interdisciplinary degrees 'out there' which should be considered. For example, if you are interested in refugee studies, consider the MSc at the Oxford Refugee Studies Centre. If you are interested in Law and Governance, consider the LLM by the same name at Queen's University Belfast. If sustainable development is your thing check out the LLM in Environmental Law at Queen Mary, and so forth.

2. Europe

Irish Centre for Human Rights, National University of Ireland, Galway
http://www.nuigalway.ie/human_rights/Programmes/llm.html

Although created in 2000, the Centre quickly established itself as a site of excellence in research and teaching in international human rights, IHL and criminal law.

University of Leiden
http://law.leiden.edu/

Leiden offers several specialized Masters programmes including in air and space law and the option of 'regular' or 'advanced' LLMs.

With its English speaking faculty and students, and ready access to research libraries and international courts and tribunals, the Netherlands is an obvious place to do an LLM in international law. Indeed, prospective students can consider most other Dutch law faculties, perhaps most notably the University of Amsterdam, for a respectable LLM in international or European law.

Vrije Universiteit Brussel
http://www.ies.be/pilc

Offering an LLM in International and European Law, VUB, as it is known, takes advantage of its position in the European capital and is highly regarded.

Other places to consider studying in Belgium include Leuven and the College of Europe in Bruges (though they are stronger in European than Public International Law per se). Kent University also has joint international Masters degrees with the Brussels School of International Studies (BSIS) if you are looking for a cross-Channel experience.

University of Lund
http://www.lu.se/lund-university/master-programmes

The Faculty of Law at Lund offers a comprehensive, two-year programme leading to a Masters in International Human Rights (with possible specializations in Intellectual Property Rights and International Labour Rights). The programme is offered in cooperation with the Raoul Wallenberg Institute of Human Rights and Humanitarian Law.

Other excellent places to do international law LLMs in the Nordic countries include the Universities of Oslo and Helsinki.

European University Institute
http://www.iue.it/LAW/ResearchTeaching/

This is a well-regarded, research-intensive Masters near Florence (yes, the location is a draw), in Comparative, European and International Law. The Institute is linguistically diverse and pan-European in orientation.

Geneva Academy of International Humanitarian Law and Human Rights
http://www.adh-geneva.ch/

The Geneva Academy, which is supported by several 'blue chip' partners, including the University of Geneva and the International Committee of the Red Cross (ICRC), offers a Masters programme in IHL. The curriculum is not exclusively IHL-focused, however, as there are courses on other branches of international law which are implicated in armed conflict, including human rights and refugee law.

3. Commonwealth

Australian National University
http://law.anu.edu.au

One of the top two or three places to study international law in Australia, the presence at this University in Canberra of the dynamic Australian Centre for International and Public Law is noteworthy.

Consider also the University of Melbourne (particularly if you have an interest in International Humanitarian or International Criminal Law), the University of Sydney and the University of New South Wales.

McGill University
http://www.mcgill.ca/law-gradprograms/

With its bilingual (though unilingual English speakers can do the LLM only in English) and bijuridical (common and civil law) traditions, McGill is perhaps the obvious place to do an LLM on international and comparative law topics in Canada. It also offers an Air and Space Law LLM.

Also in Canada, consider the University of Toronto, York University, the University of British Columbia and the Université de Montréal (particularly for French speakers), among others. Foreign students considering doing an LLM in North America should note that the tuition rates in Canada are controlled by the provinces and an LLM can be obtained at a significantly lower cost than in the US.

National Law School of India University
http://www.nls.ac.in/resources/academic_programmes_postgraduate.html

Located in Bangalore, this law school offers LLMs with human rights and business law streams (though note that some of the compulsory courses are domestically focused).

Among other international and comparative law options in India, consider the W.B. National University of Juridical Sciences in Kolkatta and the University of Delhi.

National University of Singapore
http://law.nus.edu.sg/admissions/grad_prog.html

This is probably the premiere place in Asia to undertake legal education in English. It offers numerous international and comparative law courses, and combined programmes with New York University and East China University of Politics and Law in Shanghai.

University of Cape Town
http://www.law.uct.ac.za/

A few of the South African law schools have developed particular areas of repute (Pretoria in human rights and Stellenbosch in international trade law, for example), but the University of Cape Town is a good bet for an LLM across a variety of international law areas.

Also, the University of the Western Cape has an intriguing LLM programme in Transnational Justice and Crime Prevention, in cooperation with Humboldt University in Berlin.

Victoria University of Wellington
http://www.victoria.ac.nz/law/study/postgraduate/llm

One of New Zealand's top exports to the rest of the Commonwealth appears to be legal academics. If you want to go to the source, the best places to do international law in New Zealand are Victoria, which has some highly regarded international law faculty members, and Auckland, which has a large graduate programme and hosts overseas lecturers to supplement its curriculum.

4. United States

There is a dizzying array of LLMs offered in the US, many of them very good. However, prospective applicants should be warned of both high tuition costs and a puzzling approach to graduate studies, in that LLMs have traditionally been seen as being for foreign rather than US law graduates (despite the fact that the American JD is a first degree in law). Generous funding is available at many US law schools for top LLM students.

New York University
http://www.law.nyu.edu/graduateadmissions/index.htm

NYU's School of Law is at the top of the US News and World Report ranking for international law generally (ie not specifically with respect to LLM programmes). The Faculty has several different LLM streams and at least a dozen of the 'biggest names' in international law.

American University
http://www.wcl.american.edu/ilsp/

American University Washington College of Law is particularly known for its extensive programmes in a range of international law subjects including international human rights, environmental law and trade.

Other top-ranked law schools in the field of international law are Columbia University, Harvard University, Georgetown University, Yale University and the University of Michigan-Ann Arbor.

5. Rest of the World

American University in Cairo

http://www.aucegypt.edu/GAPP/law/majmin/Pages/default.aspx

The American University in Cairo (AUC) offers an LLM in International and Comparative Law and Masters in International Human Rights Law. Fashioned on American approaches to legal education and drawing faculty from around the world, the programmes also incorporate a focus on Islamic law and the Middle East context.

Kobe University

http://www.edu.kobe-u.ac.jp/ilaw/gsics-icl/index_e.html

This university, located near Osaka, is the best place for an LLM in international law in Japan.

Consider also Kyushu University's LLM in International Economic and Business Law and the US-based Temple University's Tokyo campus.

University of Peace, Costa Rica

http://www.upeace.org/academic/masters/

The University of Peace is a United Nations University committed to interdisciplinarity. Its Masters programme in Settlement of Disputes and Human Rights is unique and offers a diverse student body.

About the Authors

Dr. Anneke Smit is Assistant Professor at the Faculty of Law, University of Windsor, Canada. She previously held a Lectureship at the School of Law, University of Reading and has been a visiting scholar at the University of Aix-Marseilles and Oxford University's Refugee Studies Centre. Dr. Smit holds a PhD from the University of Reading and an LLB from McGill University. She has held positions with the Canadian Department of Justice (Immigration and Refugee Law section), the Organization for Security and Cooperation in Europe's Mission in Kosovo, the Caucasus Institute for Peace Democracy and Development in Tbilisi, Georgia, and Citizenship and Immigration Canada and has served as a consultant on post-conflict property law to the Jerusalem Old City Initiative (JOCI). Dr. Smit's research and teaching focus on forced migration, post-conflict justice, and property law and urban planning. She is the author of *The Property and Rights of Refugees and Internally Displaced Persons: Beyond Restitution* (Routledge 2012) and co-editor with N. Valiante of *Public Interest, Private Property: Law and Planning Policy in Canada* (UBC Press, 2015).

Dr. Christopher Waters is Professor at the Faculty of Law, University of Windsor, Canada, where he teaches Public International Law and International Humanitarian Law. His previous academic post was at the School of Law, University of Reading. He has been a visiting scholar at Oxford University's Changing Character of War Programme and the University of Aix-Marseilles. Dr. Waters has extensive field experience in the Caucasus and Balkan regions with both NGOs and international organizations, including the Organization for Security and Cooperation in Europe. He is the author of *Counsel in the Caucasus* (Martinus Nijhoff 2004), *The State of Law in the South Caucasus* (Palgrave 2005), *British and Canadian Perspectives on International Law* (Martinus Nijhoff 2006), *Adjudicating International Human Rights: Essays in Honour of Sandy Ghandhi* (Martinus Nijhoff 2015), articles in the American Journal of International Law and the Canadian Yearbook of International Law, and co-editor with J.A. Green of *Conflict in the Caucasus* (Palgrave 2010).